AWS Certified Solutions Architect #1 Audio Crash Course Guide To Master Exams, Practice Test Questions, Cloud Practitioner and Security

Introduction

In this AWS Certified Solutions Architect Associate certification guide, we provide you with a comprehensive course on understanding the fundamentals of Cloud Computing, Virtualization and Autonomic Computing, which are both the new trends in IT and are expected to be the future. We define what Cloud Computing is and why it is important for any business organization to use it for better productivity or higher profits.

This book will provide you with knowledge of both public and private answer, which will be very useful in gaining enough knowledge to pass the AWS Certified Solutions Architect Associate exams. At the end of this book, you will be able to develop a cloud solution from A and Z by yourself.

This book will provide you with all the necessary information required for passing the AWS Certified Solutions Architect Associate. In this book, we have discussed all the important topics for this exam so that you can learn and test yourself before going for actual exam.

If you are currently unconvinced about why you should use AWS, keep in mind that these services offer several benefits and advantages. In using AWS, you allow the use of already familiar products—operating systems, databases, and more can be kept the same. Beyond just that, however, it is cost-effective. You don't have_to continue paying for a program that you are no longer using, nor are you required to spend massive amounts of money buying licenses for some software that you will only need very briefly. You will also see further savings simply because you will not have to spend the money on data centers and the massive costs that come along with the electricity, hardware, software, and maintenance.

1. What Is Cloud Computing?

Cloud computing is a way to cut down costs, secure data, always have access to your applications, and offer data storage as or when you need it. It is a data storage and access-sharing application/platform over the internet.

The Need for Cloud Computing

Historically, when you wanted an application, you would go and buy it off the shelf in a store. It would come in the form of a disk with an instruction manual. You would put the disk into your computer and install the program onto the computer. All data, such as pictures, spreadsheets, documents, and various files, would be stored on your computer's hard drive or some external media such as CDs, DVDs, external hard drives, SD cards, or flash drives. But there is only so much space on those devices, which ultimately means having a library full of them, depending on how much data a person has. These days, rarely anyone carries their laptop around with them since it is so much more convenient to carry a mobile device.

The Need for Personal Cloud Usage

Modern-day personal devices only have so much storage space before you have to download your data to a disk. There is nothing more annoying than needing some information but having the wrong disk or forgetting it entirely.

With all the applications in use for mobile devices, a device can run out of storage space quickly. There are extra storage add-ons a person can use, such as an extra memory card. But, as with other storage devices, the sizes are limited and only one add-on per device can be used. Mobile devices can be backed up onto computers or these extra storage devices, and if looked after, they can last. But your data is not too secure and any apps you may need instant access to will have to be reinstalled. If you need access to your data fast, it is not going to happen, as the data first has to be downloaded from the storage device. A definite need for a storage facility, where data could be stored and accessed at any time, shared with others, or shared across devices, was evident. Cloud computing was the solution since users get to choose the amount of storage they needed. People only pay for the storage they use, and they can share information across the internet and between devices. Users of cloud-based storage also have access to cloud-based applications.

The Business/Organizational Need for Cloud Computing

For companies, the need for data storage grows exponentially each year. Thus, when they are installing a networking system, they need to ensure that the system will cope for at least three years, or until their next upgrade date.

IT equipment is expensive for small, medium, and large-sized organizations. It is not only the networking infrastructure that has to be kept updated but the in-office equipment as well.

In order for the staff to be able to work efficiently and effectively, their systems need to be able to keep up with the networking equipment.

It can get even more expensive when there are staff members who constantly travel and need access to the servers.

Traveling for staff members can become burdensome if they have to carry extra drives around with them or need to be near a corporate office to be able to access the company's network.

Hosted cloud platforms are the direction in which a lot of companies are moving because they can cut down the cost of a large data center. Disaster recovery is no longer a major issue, as the systems are located in the cloud, offering more resilience.

Employees have easy and secure access to the system with nothing more than a registered PC and an internet connection. Storage is bought on an as or when required basis that does not require expensive equipment purchases.

The purchase and distribution of applications are more controlled, with a more streamlined updating procedure.

The Advantages of Cloud Computing

Cloud computing offers the following advantages for both business and personal use.

Scalable

Cloud computing offers scalable solutions that do not restrict the size, capacity, or performance of the system. If more storage is required, it is allocated on the fly and the cost added to current cloud computing capacity.

Cost-Effective

Cloud computing is cost-effective in that it can considerably cut down the costs of equipment and software. For start-up companies with limited resources or budgets, cloud computing could give the company an edge over its competitors.

Moving to cloud computing will also cut down the cost of having trained personnel to monitor, maintain, and run the systems. All the technical work is done on the side of the hosting company.

High-Speed Access and Deployment

Cloud computing provides high-speed access to your system, faster system deployment time, quicker systems downloads, and instant access to software/apps without having to do a full disk or download install.

24/7 Access From Anywhere at Anytime

The system is available 24/7, 365 days a year from anywhere in the world, as long as there is a reliable internet connection. This makes remote staffing solutions or home-based staffing solutions more simplified. Most disaster recovery procedures will have at least 12 to 48 hours of downtime before recovery, unless there is a full fallback system located off-site. Off-site disaster recovery centers are very expensive, as they require a mirror setup of the company's current system. Even systems that have these fallback centers or another off-site location may suffer data loss due to the timing of the disaster and method of data synchronization. On the other hand, when the whole system is accessed through the cloud, including shared data and applications, there is minimal chance of any data loss. The data and applications are available online from anywhere, even from a user's home, provided they have an internet connection. This makes data recovery a lot more resilient and system downtime minimal.

Systems Independence

Having a cloud-based system means that an organization is not tied down to one particular location. Moving to another location is not as costly because there are minimal systems to be moved, and there does not have to be a dedicated server or data center room. Since any device that conforms to the minimum system specifications can connect to the system, costly workstations with significantly large hard drives are no longer necessary. With the cloud acting as the network platform, as long the device is compatible with the software, data can be accessed even from an authorized smart device.

Advanced Security Features

As it is their business and the need to protect not only their system but also those of their clients, cloud hosting facilities have advanced security systems to ensure that data stays safe and secure.

Cloud Platform Models

There are four types of cloud deployment models and three types of cloud computing services. This section explains each cloud deployment method and cloud computing service.

Deployment

Choosing a deployment model is one of the first cloud computing decisions to be made. There are a few different deployment model types, but the four main ones are the most widely used ones.

A deployment model is the cloud-based environment of the customer's choice. This environment includes configuration, storage, proprietorship, costs, resources, and company needs.

Think of the deployment method as choosing a data center to outsource the companies IT networking solutions. Once a deployment method has been chosen, it makes the rest of the decisions that much easier to make.

Community Cloud

The community cloud offers similar features as that of the private cloud mixed with a few public cloud features. Yet the community cloud infrastructure is not shared with the public, but rather with several organizations that are either a subsidiary of the other, or have common goals and are known to each other.

Each organization is responsible for its own infrastructure. They will have shared resources such as software and common shared data or various mission statements, policies, etc.

The community cloud is ideal for organizations that have common interests or concerns. Examples include religious organizations, medical organizations, various scientific research centers, farming communities, and so on.

Each organization may have its own private data access, shared applications, policies, legal requirements, and shared data. This cuts down on costs, administration, and duplication of work, ensuring that any common compliances, policies, etc. are adhered to and are correct.

Hybrid Cloud

The hybrid cloud is made up of two or more of the deployment cloud methods. This method is the most flexible out of all the methods, as it offers an organization the ability to share public resources, share community resources with a selected group, and still keep their sensitive data or any proprietary software private.

Private Cloud

The private cloud is for the sole use of one organization. All resources, shared data, and sensitive data are accessible only by the organization that controls the private cloud. It is not the most cost-efficient solution, but it offers the greatest security, reliability, and stability out of all the deployment models.

Public Cloud

This is the deployment method that is most widely used and is broadly considered as "the cloud." It is used by both individuals and businesses who are in need of shared resources. It is the most cost-effective of all the cloud deployment methods and requires the least security.

The services that are used can be pay-per-use, but the cloud is managed by the third-party company that owns the cloud.

Applications

Cloud computing offers three different types of services, each offering a company or end-user different components. The service required will depend on the consumer's needs, whether they are a business or an end-user.

Software as a Service

This is the most popular service model for cloud computing, used by both end-users and businesses. The service is managed completely by the cloud service provider. The cloud service provider hosts a number of applications, which are made available to end-users or businesses that are signed up for the SaaS model.

SaaS is the public transport of the services. It is convenient, cost-effective, and you get where you want to go. But you are limited to their routes, time frame, and service providers. Public transport is used by thousands of others, all taking the same public transport as you do. Still, you get to choose which transportation you use (scaled to the costs that suit your pocket) and the routes you want to use.

SaaS is also the easiest out of all the service models to use and comes with pay-per-use options, which makes it attractive for the personal-use sector or smaller businesses.

Platform as a Service (PaaS)

Platform as a Service (PaaS) is mostly used by developers that design applications. It is also used for various companies that offer services.

PaaS is like using a regular taxi service company. You have control over which car you would like to suit your transport needs. You have control over your destination, and even on your route. Although you don't share the taxi at the same time as others, it is still a shared resource.

The operating system, storage, networking, virtualization, runtime, and middleware are all offered as a service. These services are managed with pooled resources which the consumer/business has no control over. They are offered as a service by the service provider, so any changes or additions will be controlled by the service provider.

Data and applications are managed by the consumer or business, which means they have complete control over them. PaaS offers the consumer or business partial control over the hosted services.

Infrastructure as a Service (IaaS)

IaaS offers infrastructure as a service and is for companies or organizations that need a more secure environment for their data. Organizations that choose IaaS have complete autonomy over the software, operating system, storage, and so on. Some large-scale organizations may even choose to host their own cloud-based solutions.

IaaS is more like a long-term lease or rental car. The business may not own the car outright, but they have almost full control over it. An added benefit is that there are minimal to no maintenance costs on the 'car,' as that is done by the lease or rental agency. Plus the 'car' can go just about anywhere without restricted routes or having to conform to public or taxi transport rules. Your space is completely your own and not shared by the public or other businesses.

IaaS offers the consumer or business significantly more control over the hosted services than SaaS and PaaS.

Talk about what Cloud Computing is, the basics of server visualization.

Characteristics

Broad community access: Capabilities can be found with the network and can be accessed via regular mechanisms that promote usage by heterogeneous thin or maybe heavy customer platforms (e.g., tablets, mobile phones, workstations, and laptops).

Resource pooling: The provider's computing methods are pooled to deliver numerous customers with a multi-tenant design, with various physical as well as virtual resources dynamically assigned and reassigned based on customer demand. There's a feeling of location independence in which the customer generally has no knowledge or control over the actual location of the provided energy, but might be ready to specify location at a greater degree of abstraction (e.g., nation, datacenter or state). Instances of materials include storage, network bandwidth, memory, and processing.

Fast elasticity: Capabilities might be elastically provisioned as well as released in a number of instances instantly, to scale outward as well as inward quickly. For the customer, the skills offered for provisioning usually seem to be limitless and can be appropriated in any amount anytime.

Measured service: Cloud methods automatically manage and enhance source usage by leveraging a metering capability in some amount of abstraction, acceptable on the service type (e.g., processing, storage, bandwidth along with energetic user accounts). Resource usage could be monitored, controlled as well as reported, offering transparency for the provider as well as the consumer.

Cloud platform models and talk about the characteristics of the Cloud and their application.

2. AWS Certified Solutions Architect Associate (SAA-CO2)

The AWS Certified Solutions Architect Associate (SAA-CO2) is not an easy exam to pass, and the student needs to put a good few months of hard preparation and study into passing it. The tester must go over their work several times, making sure they fully understand the content.

It will also help a great deal if the student can work in a lab environment to get hands-on experience with the study material. Although the student may already work in an AWS environment, it is best to keep learning in a controlled lab type environment. For the sake of the course and exam, they require students to assess and answer questions based on various scenarios. It is safe to say, while they may build these situations around real-word ones, they will not mimic any live environments the student may work in.

Different Ways to Take the Course

To do the course you can sign up with Amazon at the following website link:

https://aws.amazon.com/certification/certified-solutions-architect-associate/

For more information on how the course will run, you can get this information from the following website link:

https://aws.amazon.com/certification/certification-prep/

Creating an AWS account is quick, simple, and free of charge. There are, however, some fees involved for specific courses, exams, or exam simulators offered by AWS.

Benefits of Becoming an AWS Certified Solutions Architect Associate (SAA-Co2)

There are numerous benefits for becoming an AWS Certified Solutions Architect Associate for both the IT professional or aspiring IT professional.

These benefits include:

- Better career opportunities
- Career advancement opportunities
- Higher pay structure
- Demonstrates the holder of the certificate's expertise in the field
- Gives the IT professional more credibility

- Makes an IT resume stand out from the rest

What to Expect

The course covers all the basic material that the learner will find in the materials they receive. The best route is a classroom-based course that covers:

- AWS Technical Essentials
- Architecting on AWS
- Architecting on AWS - Accelerator

AWS also offers the Exam Readiness training, which can be done as either:

- Classroom training—This is given either a virtual or physical classroom training environment with an accredited and certified AWS instructor.
- Digital training—This can be taken through AWS, and the learner can take the course as it suits them.
- Webinars—An AWS-accredited instructor leads scheduled webinars with question and answer sessions after the webinar is done.

This book will help you:

- Identify key topics that are required for the exam from each of the four domains.
- Read questions and identify keywords before choosing an answer during the exam.
- Practice the exam with actual exam-type questions.

The Goal of the AWS Certified Solutions Architect

The course is designed to teach cloud solutions architects how to create architectures that fill the requirements of the 4 AWS Domains covered in this course.

By the end of the course and exam, the cloud solutions architect must be able to create AWS architectures that are:

- Resilient
- Performant
- Secure
- Cost-optimized

- Offer operation excellence

Exams

There are 65 questions when taking the SAA-CO2 exam for which you have 130 minutes to complete. The exam is scored from 100 to 1000 points, and the student needs to have scored 720 or higher to pass.

If the exam is not passed, it can be taken again five days after the previous exam. Upon successful completion of the exam, the certification is valid for two years, after which recertification is required at a reduced cost to the student.

The following are where the exam can be taken and each facility has test simulators for the SAA-CO2:

- AWS — https://www.aws.training/certification
- Pearsons VUE - https://home.pearsonvue.com/aws/onvue

AWS SAA-CO2 Exam Question Allocation Table Content Outline

The exam has the following content domains that each make up a percentage of the exam:

Domain 1: Design Resilient Architectures, which makes up 30% of the exams.

This domain consists of the following topics or concepts for resilient AWS architectures:

- The learner must be able to design a multi-tier architecture solution.
- The learner must be able to design highly available and fault-tolerant architectures.
- Using AWS service, the learner must be able to design decoupling mechanisms.
- The learning is required to know how to choose appropriate resilient storage.

Domain 2: Design High-Performing Architectures which makes up 28% of the exams.

This domain consists of the following topics or concepts pertaining to a workload:

- Identify scalable and elastic compute solutions for a workload.
- Select scalable and high-performing storage solutions for a workload.
- Select networking solutions based on high-performance for a workload.
- Select database solutions for a workload that are high-performance.

Domain 3: Design Secure Applications and Architectures, which makes up 24% of the exams.

This domain consists of the following topics or concepts about security:

- The learner must be able to design secure access to AWS resources.
- The learners must understand and be able to design secure application tiers.
- The learner must be confident enough to select appropriate data security options.

Domain 4: Design Cost-Optimized Architectures which makes up 18% of the exams.

This domain consists of the following topics or concepts about cost-optimization of AWS:

- This domain requires the student to be able to identify cost-effective storage solutions.
- The student must know how to identify database services and compute cost-effective services.
- The student must be able to expertly design cost-effective network architectures.

What to Expect From the Exam

To do well and pass the exam, the student is expected to know the AWS core services and how to use them to create systems that follow AWS best practices.

Every missed answer is marked as an incorrect answer, and an incorrect answer will bring down the overall score of the exam.

A question can be marked for future consideration, but try and guess what you think it may be before moving on to the next question. That way, if time runs out and you have not had a chance to go back to review the question, you have a chance of getting it right as opposed to not answering it at all.

At the end of the exam, you can review each answer and questions you have marked for review. Marking a question for review also makes it easier to get back to, especially when time is running short.

It is important to keep an eye on the time periodically throughout the exam, and if you feel you are spending too much time on a question, mark it for review rather than keep going back to it.

The exam content will contain questions that are broken down into Response Types and Unscored Content.

When taking the exams, it is vital to remember that all the details on the test questions may count.

Response Types

The examination is broken down into two types of questions that will be asked of the student. These questions are:

- Multiple choice questions—These questions only have one correct answer but the student will be given a choice of four answers to choose from. The three incorrect answers are what are known as distractor answers.

Example:

Q1: What is the color of the sky?

A. Orange

B. Green

C. Azure

D. Lemon

Answer: C. Azure

- Multiple response questions—These types usually have one question with 5 to 6 answers to choose from. It will be stated how many correct answers to choose from the list of given answers. For instance, the question may say something like, from the following list, choose the two correct answers.

Example:

Q2: What are the parts of a motor car?

Choose two.

A. Seat

B. Jar

C. Engine

D. Lid

E. Bag

Answer: A. Seat & C. Engine

Not all of the questions will be ones that have obvious answers that stand out. Some of the questions will require the exam taker to choose the right procedure or solution for the scenario put forward in the matter.

Example:

Q3: Mary needs to make some toast with butter and jam. From the options below, choose the procedure that best explains how to make the buttered toast.

A. Put the bread on the plate and butter it with fresh butter.

B. Put the butter and bread on the plate with a knife.

C. Put the bread and butter in the oven on high for 20 minutes.

D. Put the bread in the toaster, and when it pops out, put it on a plate and butter the bread.

Answer: D. Put the bread in the toaster and when it pops out, put it on a plate and butter the bread.

Work through the questions by eliminating answers that you are sure do not pertain to the question. If you know the subject well enough, the incorrect answers will be more clear. There are always two answers that will look pretty similar. They need to be read through really carefully because this is what trips a student up.

Unscored Content

There may be what is called unscored content included on the exam. Although they do not affect the exam takers score they are there to gather statistical information.

End of the Exam

It is a good idea to flag questions you had doubts about, so if you have time at the end of the exam you can review them.

At the end of the exam, the student will receive their mark and whether or not they passed the exam. They will also get the statistics on what their strengths and weaknesses were for the subject based on answers.

Whether the student passes or fails the exam, the strength and weakness table is a valuable tool. It will show the learner what they need to work on within the AWS domain to continue focusing on.

Do not let it discourage you if you did not pass the first time around, not many people do. But you will know what you need to go back and work on to ensure you do pass the next time around.

How to Choose the Best Answer for Exam Questions

This section will cover some question strategies that will help the student identify and consider when choosing an answer to exam questions.

If you find you do not understand or recognize a concept, system, or core service during practice tests, go back and study it. A term, idea, or service you are not familiar with is a sure sign that you are not ready to take the full exam. This is one of the reasons exam simulators and practice tests are so important to any student.

It is also good to realize that practice tests and test simulations are not going to be exactly the same as the exam. But the way in which you need to strategize the answers and the thought process that goes into each question will be the same.

Good Exam Answering Strategy:

- Before answering, read both the questions and answers through and make sure you understand it.

- Look for key features that may match both the question and the answer.

- Rule out any answer that you know for certain does not pertain to or could be the correct answer. Leave only those answers that may have some bearing on the question.

- Always pay attention to qualifying clauses as these are put there to see if the test taker is paying attention to detail. For instance, the question may be for the most cost-effective, efficient solution, which is not always the most suitable. If a company is tightening up on costs, they may not always be looking for the best solution but the one that offers them the most value.

- If the answer pertains to AWS core services, look for clues in the question.

3. Easy Storage Service from Amazon (Amazon S3) and Storage for Amazon Glacier

This chapter will help you understand Amazon Simple Storage Service (Amazon S3) and Amazon Glacier, the main object storage services available on AWS.

Amazon S3 offers stable, reliable and extremely scalable cloud storage for developers and IT teams. With a simple web service interface, Amazon S3 is a simple-to-use object storage that can be used to store and retrieve any amount of data, anywhere on the Internet. Amazon S3 also enables you pay only for the storage you use, eliminating the capacity planning and capacity constraints associated with traditional storage.

Amazon S3 was among the first services introduced by AWS. It serves as one of the most important web services: almost all applications run on AWS using Amazon S3, whether directly or indirectly. Amazon S3 can be used alone or in combination with other AWS services, as with many other AWS cloud services as it provides a very wide range of integration. For instance, for Amazon Kinesis and Amazon Elastic MapReduce (Amazon EMR) snapshots, Amazon S3 serves as the durable target storage and it is used as the snapshot storage for Amazon Elastic Block Store (Amazon EBS) and Amazon Relational Database Service (Amazon RDS). Furthermore, it is used as a data storage platform or loading mechanism for Amazon Redshift and Amazon DynamoDB, among many other functions. Due to the flexibility of Amazon S3 and its high integration level and usability, it's important to understand the service in detail.

Common usage scenarios for Amazon S3 storage are:

- Data backup and archiving on-premises or in the cloud
- Storage and distribution of content, media and software
- Big data analysis
- Static website hosting
- Hosting of native mobile and internet applications in the cloud
- Disaster recovery

To support these and more usage options, Amazon S3 offers a range of storage classes designed for a variety of common use scenerios: general use, infrequent access, and archiving. To help manage data throughout its lifecycle, Amazon S3 offers configurable lifecycle policies. By using these lifecycle policies, you can automatically migrate your data to the most suitable storage class, without changing your application code. To control who can access your data, Amazon S3 offers a comprehensive set of permissions, access controls, and encryption options.

Amazon Glacier is another cloud storage service linked to Amazon S3 but optimized for data archiving and long-term backup at an extremely low cost. Amazon Glacier is suitable for "cold data," that is, data that is not requested often and for which a recovery time of three to five hours is acceptable. Amazon Glacier can be used both as an Amazon S3 storage class (see Storage Classes and Object Lifecycle Management in the Amazon S3 Advanced Features section) and as an independent archiving storage service (see Amazon Glacier section).

Traditional Block and File Storage versus Object Storage

In traditional computing environments, two types of storage dominate: bulk storage and file storage. Block storage operates at a lower level - the raw storage device level - and manages data as a set of numbered blocks of fixed size. File storage functions at a higher level (level of the operating system) and handles data as a named file and folder hierarchy. Block and file storage is often network-accessible in the form of a Storage Area Network (SAN) for block storage, using protocols such as iSCSI or Fiber Channel, or as a Network Attached Storage (NAS) file server or "filer" for file storage, using protocols such as Common Internet File System (CIFS) or Network File System (NFS). Whether directly attached or connected to the network, bulk or file, this type of storage is closely related to the server and operating system that uses the storage.

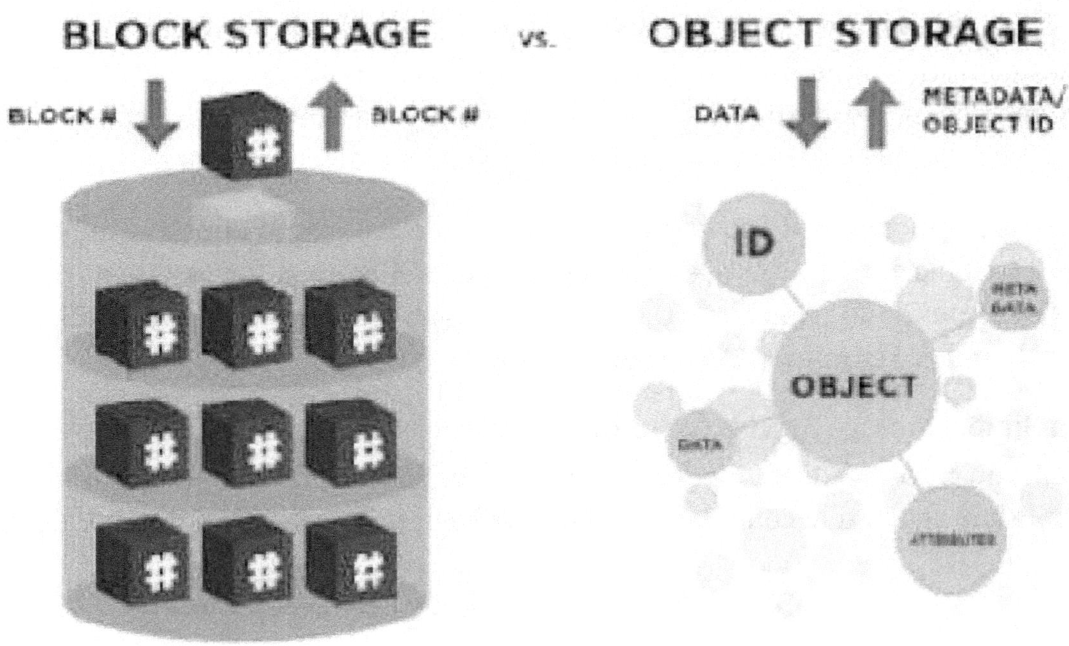

Saving Amazon S3 objects is quite another form. Amazon S3 is used for object storage in the cloud. Rather than being closely tied to a server, Amazon S3 storage is server-independent and accessible from the Internet. Rather than managing data as blocks or files with SCSI, CIFS or NFS protocols, data is managed as objects using an application program interface (API) based on standard HTTP verbs.

Both data and metadata can be found in any Amazon S3 object. Objects reside in containers called buckets, and a specific user-specified key (filename) identifies each object. Buckets are plain flat folder with no hierarchy in the file system. You can possess several buckets but you cant own a sub bucket. An infinite number of things can carry any bucket.

An Amazon S3 object is easy to illustrate, like a file and the Key as a file name. Bear in mind, however, that Amazon S3 is not a conventional file system and varies substantially. You GET an object or Place an object on Amazon S3, then, you can work on the entire object at once instead of incrementally updating parts of the object like you would with a file. You cannot "mount" a bucket, "open" an object, install an operating system on Amazon S3, or run a database on it.

Rather than a file system, Amazon S3 is very durable and highly scalable object storage optimized for reading and designed with an intentionally minimalist feature set. It provides a simple and robust file storage abstraction that frees you from many of the underlying details that you would normally encounter in traditional storage.

You don't have to worry about durability or data replication between availability zones - Amazon S3 objects are automatically replicated to multiple devices across multiple installations in the same region. The same goes for scalability: if your request speed is steadily increasing, Amazon S3 automatically distributes buckets to support very fast request speeds and also allows simultaneous access by many customers.

AWS provide options for a conventional block or file storage in addition to Amazon S3 storage. The Amazon EBS service provides block-level storage for instances of Amazon Elastic Compute Cloud (Amazon EC2). Amazon Elastic File System (AWS EFS) provides network shared file storage (NAS storage) using the NFS v4 protocol.

Amazon Simple Storage Service (Amazon S3) Basics

Now that you have the basic understanding of some of the major differences between two simple storage in the cloud, let's explore the basics of Amazon S3 in more detail.

Buckets

A bucket is a container (web folder) stored on Amazon S3 for objects (files). A bucket normally consists of an Amazon S3 object. For Amazon S3, buckets are the top-level namespace, and bucket names are always global. This implies that, much like the Domain Name System (DNS) domain names, and not just within your account, your bucket names must be identical to all AWS accounts. Up to 63 numbers, lowercase letters, hyphens and periods can be used to create bucket names. You can create and use multiple compartments and you can also have up to 100 per standard account.

It is highly recommended to use bucket names containing your domain name and which also comply with the DNS name rules. This ensures that your bucket names are yours, can be used in all regions, and can also host static websites.

AWS Regions

Although the Amazon S3 bucket namespace is global, each Amazon S3 bucket is created in a specific region of your choice. This allows you to monitor where you store your data. To reduce latency, you can build and use buckets that are near a specific collection of end-users or customers, or in a particular region to address data location and sovereignty issues, or away from your core facilities to enable disaster compliance recovery and compliance needs. You can also determine the location of your data; data from an Amazon S3 bucket can be stored in that region unless you explicitly copy it to another bucket in a different region.

Objects

In Amazon S3 containers, objects are the entities or files stored. In any format, an object can store nearly any type of data. Item sizes can vary from 0 to 5 TB bytes, and an infinite number of objects can be found in a single bucket. This implies that Amazon S3 can save an almost infinite amount of data.

Furthermore, an object is made up of data (the file itself) and metadata (the file data). An Amazon S3 object's data section is invisible to the Amazon S3. This means that the data of an object can be treated as a single stream of bytes. Amazon S3 doesn't know or care about what type of data you are storing, and the service doesn't work differently for text data and binary data.

A list of name/value pairs that can be used to identify the object is similar to the metadata associated with an Amazon S3 object. There are two kinds of metadata: metadata from the device and metadata from the user. Amazon S3 itself generates and uses device metadata and includes items such as last updated date, object size, MD5 digest, and a form of HTTP content. User metadata is optional and can be defined when an object is being created. You can tag the data with attributes that are relevant to you using custom metadata.

Keys

A unique identifier called a key identifies each object stored in a S3 bucket. The Key can be thought of as a file name. A key can contain up to 1024 bytes of Unicode UTF-8 characters, including built-in slashes, backslashes, periods, and hyphens.

Keys must be unique within the same compartment, but different compartments can contain similar Key. The bucket, Key, and optional version ID combination can be used to uniquely identify an Amazon S3 object.

Object URL

Amazon S3 is a storage for web, and each Amazon S3 object can be addressed by a unique URL that is the web services endpoint, bucket name, Key and object. For instance, with the URL:

- HTTP:/mybucket.s3.amazonaws.com / jack.doc Mybucket is the S3 bucket's name, and the main or file name is jack.doc. If a different object is made, such as:
- HTTP:/mybucket.s3.amazonaws.com / fee / fi / fog / smoke / jack.doc.com then, the bucket name is still mybucket but now the key or filename is string.
- fresh / fi / fo / fum / jack.doc. A key can contain delimiting characters such as forward slashes or backslashes that can help you name and logically organize your Amazon S3 objects, but for Amazon S3, it involves just a long key name in a flat namespace. There is no real hierarchy of files and folders. For more information, see the "Prefixes and Separators" topic in the "Amazon S3 Advanced Features" section that follows.

For added convenience, the Amazon S3 console and the Prefix and Separator feature lets you navigate an Amazon S3 bucket as if they were arranged in folders' hierarchy. Note, however, that a bucket with unorganized keys is a single, flat namespace.

Operations of Amazon S3

The Amazon S3 API, with only a handful of common edits, is easy to use. They include:

- Creating/deleting a bucket
- Write an Entity
- Reading an object
- Delete an item
- List of keys inside a compartment

REST Interface

A REST API (Representational State Transfer) is the native interface for Amazon S3. With the REST interface, you can use regular HTTP or HTTPS requests to build and delete buckets, list keys, and read and write objects. By default, REST maps HTTP "verbs" (HTTP methods) to typical CRUD operations (Create, Read, Update, Delete). Create is HTTP PUT (and sometimes POST); reading is HTTP GET; delete is HTTP DELETE, and the update is HTTP POST.

For quality assurance to ensure that your requests and data are safe, always use HTTPS for Amazon S3 API requests.

Users do not explicitly apply the REST interface in most situations but communicate with Amazon S3 through one of the available top-level interfaces. These include the AWS SDKs (wrapper libraries) for iOS, Android, JavaScript, Java, .NET, Node.js, PHP, Python, Ruby, Go and C ++, the interface command line (CLI), and the AWS Management Console.

Amazon S3 originally supported a Simple Object Access Protocol (SOAP) API in addition to the REST API, but you must apply the REST API. The old HTTPS endpoint is still available, but new features are not supported.

Durability and Availability

Durability and data availability are related, but are slightly different concepts. Sustainability answers the question, "Will my data still be available in the future?" Availability answers the question, "Can I access my data now?" Amazon S3 is designed to deliver your data with high degree of reliability and availability.

In a given year, Amazon S3 Standard Storage is built for 99.99999999999 per cent longevity and 99.99 per cent item availability. For example, if you store 10,000 Amazon S3 objects, on average, you can expect the loss of one object every 10,000,000 years. By automatically storing data redundantly across multiple devices in multiple installations and in the same area, Amazon S3 can achieve high durability. It is designed to withstand simultaneous data loss in two installations without losing user data. Amazon S3 offers a highly durable storage infrastructure designed for the storage of critical and primary data.

Suppose you want to store non-critical or easily reproducible derived data (such as thumbnail of images) that do not require this high level of durability, you can use Reduced Redundancy Storage (RRS) for a low fee. RRS offers 99.99% durability with a lower storage cost than traditional Amazon S3 storage.

Although Amazon S3 storage offers very high durability at the infrastructural level, it is still recommended to provide protection against accidental deletion or overwriting of data at the user level by taking advantage of additional monitoring features which include Version control, cross-regional replication and removal of MFA.

Data Consistency

Amazon S3 is ultimately a cohesive system. As your data is automatically replicated to multiple servers and locations in a region, it can take a longer period of time for your data changes to propagate to all other locations. Therefore, in this situation, the information you read immediately after an update can result in outdated data.

This is no problem in using PUTs for new objects: in this case, Amazon S3 offers read-after-write consistency. However, to use PUTs for existing objects (overwrite object to an existing key) and for DELETE objects, Amazon S3 provides final consistency.

Any consistency means that if you put new data on an existing key, a subsequent GET can return the old data. Likewise, if you DELETE an object, another GET for that object can still read the deleted object. Either way, single key updates are atomic - for consistent reads to the end, you can obtain new data or old data, but never an inconsistent mix of data.

Access Control

Amazon S3 is secured by default; when you create a bucket or an object in Amazon S3, only you can have access to it. To enable you grant others controlled access, Amazon S3 provides both coarse-grained access controls (Amazon S3 access control lists [ACL]) and fine-grained access-controls (Amazon S3 Bucket Policies, AWS Identity and Access Management (IAM) Policies and Query String Authentication).

Amazon S3 ACLs allow you to grant such coarse-grained permissions at an object or bucket level: READ, WRITE, or FULL CONTROL. ACLs are an old system of access control produced before IAM existed. Today, ACLs are best used for a limited number of usage cases, such as enabling bucket logging or creating a bucket that hosts a static, globally readable website.

In place of a primary IAM, they are connected to the bucket resource. They include in the policy, an explicit reference to the primary IAM. This principle can be associated with another AWS account so that you can assign multi-account access to Amazon S3 resources using Amazon S3 Bucket Policy.

With an Amazon S3 bucket policy, you can decide who can access the bucket, from where (by classless cross-domain routing block [CIDR] or IP address) and at a particular time of day.

Finally, IAM policies can be directly associated with primary IAMs that grant access to an Amazon S3 bucket, just as they can offer any AWS service and resource access. Clearly, you can only delegate IAM policies to AWS account customers that you control.

Static Website Hosting

A common usage case for Amazon S3 storage involves hosting static websites. Many websites, especially microsites, do not require the services of a full web server. A static website means that all pages on the website contain only static content and do not require any processing on the server such as PHP, ASP.NET or JSP. (Note that this doesn't mean that the website cannot be interactive and dynamic; it can be achieved with client-side scripting such as JavaScript embedded in static HTML web pages.) There are several benefits to static websites: they are very fast, highly scalable and are more secure than a traditional dynamic website. Hosting a static website on Amazon S3 can also take advantage of the security, durability, availability and scalability of Amazon S3.

Since every Amazon S3 object has a URL, converting a bucket into a website is relatively easy. To host a static website, you need to configure a bucket for website hosting and then upload the static website content to the bucket.

To configure an Amazon S3 bucket to host static websites:

- Create a bucket with the same name as the hostname of the desired website.
- Download the static files to the bucket.
- Make all files public (readable worldwide).
- Enable static website hosting for the bucket. This includes specifying an index document and an error document.
- The website is now available at the S3 website URL: <bucket-name> .s3-website-<AWS-region> .amazonaws.com.
- Create a friendly DNS name in your own domain for the website using CNAME DNS or an Amazon Route 53 alias that matches the Amazon S3 website URL.
- The website is now available under the domain name of your website.

Amazon S3 Advanced Functions

Also, for the basics, there are some advanced features of Amazon S3 that you should also familiarize yourself with..

Prefixes and Separators

Although Amazon S3 uses a flat structure in a bucket, it supports the use of prefix and separator parameters when listing key names. This functionality allows you to organize, browse, and retrieve the objects in a bucket in a hierarchical manner. Typically, you should use a forward slash (/) or a backslash (\) as a separator and then, use key names with embedded separators to emulate a hierarchy of files and folders in the key namespace. a flat object of a compartment.

For example, you want to store a series of server logs by server name (such as server42), but organized by year and month, as follows:

Logs / January 2016 / Server42.logs

Logs / February / 2016 / server42.log

Logs / 2016 / March / 42.log server

The REST API, the Encapsulation SDKs, the AWS CLI, and the Amazon Management Console all support the use of separators and prefixes. This feature allows you to organize new data logically and easily manage the hierarchical folder and file structure of existing data downloaded or backed up from traditional file systems. When used with IAM or Amazon S3 bucket policies, prefixes and delimiters can also help create the equivalent of department "subfolders" or "home directories" of users in a single bucket, restricting or sharing access to those "subfolders" (defined by prefixes) as required.

Use object separators and prefixes to organize objects in your Amazon S3 buckets hierarchically, but keep in mind that Amazon S3 is really not a filesystem.

Storage Classes

Amazon S3 provides a number of storage classes that are sufficient for various usage cases.

Amazon S3 Standard provides high reliability, high availability, low latency and high-quality object storage for general use. As it offers low latency in the first byte and high throughput, the Standard is preferable for short or long term storage of frequently used data. For most general usage cases, it is best to start with Amazon S3 Standard.

The Amazon S3 Standard-Infrequent Access (Standard-IA) provides the same longevity, low latency, and high performance as the Amazon S3 Standard, but it is designed for long-life data and less-accessed data. Standard-IA has a lower storage cost per GB monthly than the Standard, but the pricing model also includes a minimum object size (128 KB), the minimum duration (30 days), and recovery cost per GB, so it is best suited to rarely access data stored for more than 30 days.

Reduced Redundancy Storage (RRS) from Amazon S3 provides slightly lower reliability (4 new) at a reduced cost than Normal or Normal-IA. It is most suitable for derived data, such as image thumbnails, that can be easily replicated.

Finally, for data that does not require real-time access, such as archives and long-term backups, the Amazon Glacier storage class provides reliable, robust and highly cost-effective cloud storage. To keep costs down, Amazon Glacier is optimized for minimally-used data with a recovery time of several hours. To restore an Amazon Glacier object, issue a restore command with one of the Amazon S3 APIs; three to five hours later, the Amazon Glacier object is then copied to Amazon S3 RRS. Note that the restore option will simply make a copy on the Amazon S3 RRS; the original data object remains in Amazon Glacier until it is explicitly deleted. Also, it is important to note that Amazon Glacier allows you to retrieve up to 5% of the Amazon S3 data stored in Amazon Glacier for free every month. For restorations outside the daily meal allowance, costs for delivery has been made available.

Amazon Glacier is not only used as a storage tier in Amazon S3, but it is also a stand-alone storage service with a separate API and unique functions. However, when you use Amazon Glacier as the Amazon S3 storage class, you can still communicate with data through Amazon S3 APIs. See the Amazon Glacier section for details.

Set a data recovery policy to limit recovery for the free tier or to a maximum limit of GB per hour to avoid or minimize Amazon Glacier recovery costs.

Object Lifecycle Management

Managing the lifecycle of Amazon S3 objects is roughly equivalent to exhausting automated storage in the traditional IT storage infrastructures. In many cases, data has a natural life cycle, starting with "hot" (frequently accessed) data, moving to "hot" (less frequently accessed) data as it ages, and ending with "hot" data. It then moves to Cold" data (backup or long-term archive) before possible deletion.

For example, many business documents are often viewed as they are created, and are hardly viewed over time. In many cases, however, compliance rules require that business records be archived and kept accessible for years. Likewise, studies show that file, operating system, and database backups are most often opened within the first few days of being created, usually to remove an accidental error. After a week or two, these backups will remain a critical asset, but they are much less likely to be accessible for recovery. Compliance laws require a variety of copies to be held for many years in many cases.

With the use of Amazon S3 lifecycle configuration rules, you can reduce your storage costs by automatically transferring data from one storage class to another or even automatically removing the data after a period of time. For example, the backup data lifecycle rules can be:

- Initially saving the backup data in Amazon S3 Standard.
- Switching to Amazon Standard-IA after 30 days.
- After 90 days, begin transition to Amazon Glacier.
- Remove after 3 years.

Lifecycle configurations are linked to the bucket and can apply to all objects in the bucket or only objects specified with a prefix.

Encryption

Encrypting all confidential data contained in Amazon S3, both in flight and at rest, is highly suggested.

Amazon S3 Stable Sockets Layer (SSL) API endpoints can be used to encrypt the Amazon S3 data on the fly. This implies that when in transit over HTTPS, all data sent to and from Amazon S3 is encrypted.

You can use multiple server-side encryption (SSE) variants to encrypt your Amazon S3 data at rest. Amazon S3 encrypts the data at the object level as it writes it to its data centers' drives, and decrypts it for you as you access it. All SSEs run by Amazon S3 and AWS Key Management Service (Amazon KMS) use the advanced 256-bit encryption standard (AES). You can also use client-side encryption to encrypt your Amazon S3 data when at rest, where your data is encrypted for the client before it is sent to Amazon S3.

SSE-S3 (AWS managed keys)
It is a fully integrated "checkbox" encryption solution in which AWS manages key management and key protection for Amazon S3. With a unique key, each object is encrypted. A separate master key then encrypts the real object key itself. At least once a month, a new master key is released, with AWS running the keys. On secure hosts, encrypted data, encryption keys, and master keys are all stored separately, further improving security.

SSE-KMS (AWS KMS keys)
It is a fully integrated solution where Amazon manages and protects your keys for Amazon S3, but you can manage the keys. SSE-KMS offers several additional advantages over SSE-S3. There are different permissions required to access the master key by using SSE-KMS, and this helps to prevent unauthorized access to your Amazon S3 stored items and also adds an additional layer of control. AWS KMS also offers

auditing, so you are familiar with whoever is using the key to access objects and time of object access. AWS KMS also allows you to view all unsuccessful attempts to access data by users who were not allowed to decrypt the information.

SSE-C (keys provided by the customer)

This is used if you want to keep your own encryption keys, but don't want to manage or deploy your own client-side encryption library. With SSE-C, AWS performs encryption/ decryption of your objects while retaining full control over the keys used to encrypt/ decrypt the objects in Amazon S3.

Client-Side Encryption

Client-side encryption refers to the process of encrypting the data on the client-side of your application before it is sent to Amazon S3. To use data encryption keys, you can follow these options:

- Use a customer master key managed by AWS KMS.
- Use a master key on the client-side.

When you use client-side encryption, you retain full control of the encryption process, including the management of encryption keys.

You can also use server-side encryption with keys operated by AWS (SSE-S3 or SSE-KMS) for optimum flexibility and ease of use.

Versioning

By maintaining different versions of an object in the bucket, marked by a unique version ID, Amazon S3 Versioning helps protect the data from unintentional or intentional deletion. Versioning allows any version of an object stored in your Amazon S3 bucket to be preserved, retrieved, and restored. If a user makes a change unintentionally or even deletes an object in your S3 bucket maliciously, you can restore the object back to its source by simply referring to the version ID next to the bucket and the key.

Versioning at the level of the bucket is allowed. Until this is allowed, it is not possible to delete the version from the bucket as it cannot be suspended.

MFA Delete

MFA Delete adds an extra layer of data protection in addition to bucket version management. MFA Delete requires additional authentication to permanently delete an object version or change the version control status of a bucket. MFA Delete requires an authentication code created by a hardware or virtual appliance multi-factor authentication (MFA), in addition to your usual security credentials. Please note that the root account can only enable MFA deletion.

Pre-signed URLs

All Amazon S3 objects are private by default. This means that only the owner has access. However, by creating a pre-signed URL, the object owner may optionally share objects with other individuals, using their own security credentials to grant time-limited permission to download the objects. When creating a predefined URL for your object, you must provide your security credentials and provide a bucket name, object key, HTTP method (GET to download the object). Pre-signed URLs are only valid for the specified length of time. This is especially useful in forming protection against "content scraping" of web content, such as media files stored in Amazon S3.

Multipart Upload

To further support the downloading or copying of large objects, Amazon S3 provides the multipart download API. This allows you to download large objects in parts, as it generally provides better network usage (via parallel transfers), the ability to pause and resume, and the ability to download objects with unknown sizes. .

Multipart download is a three-step process: start, share, download, and finish (or abort). The parts can be downloaded independently in any order, possibly with retransmission. After all, parts are uploaded, Amazon S3 assembles the parts to create an object.

In general, you should use a multipart download for objects larger than 100MB, and objects larger than 5GB. If you are using low-level APIs, you need to download the file in parts and keep track of the parts. When using the high-level APIs and high-level Amazon S3 commands in the AWS CLI (AWS s3 cp, AWS s3 mv and AWS s3 sync), the multipart Upload is automatically required for large objects.

You can set up an object lifecycle policy for a bucket to prevent incomplete multiple downloads after a specified number of days. This minimizes the storage costs associated with multipart downloads that have not been completed.

Range GET

It is possible to download only part of an object (GET) in Amazon S3 and Amazon Glacier using the Range GET. By using the HTTP range header in the GET request or equivalent parameters in one of the SDK wrapper libraries, you can specify the byte range for the object. This can be useful in dealing with large objects if you have a bad connection, or for downloading only a known portion of a large Amazon Glacier backup.

Interregional Replication

Interregional Replication is a feature on Amazon S3 that allows you to asynchronously replicate all new objects from the source bucket in one AWS region to a target bucket in another region. All metadata and ACLs associated with the object are also part of the replication. After configuring cross-regional replication on your source bucket, any change to an object's data, metadata, or ACL will trigger a new replication to the target bucket. To enable cross-regional replication, versioning must be enabled for the source and target buckets, and you must use an IAM policy to allow Amazon S3 replicate objects on your behalf.

Cross-regional replication is often used to reduce the latency required to access objects in Amazon S3 by moving the objects closer to a group of users or to meet the requirements for storing backup data outside the source data. If enabled in an existing bucket, replication between regions will only replicate new objects. Existing objects are not replicated and must be copied to the new compartment via a separate command.

Logging

You can enable Amazon S3 server access logs to monitor requests for your Amazon S3 bucket.

By default, Logout is disabled but can be easily allowed. When you allow bucket logging (the source bucket), you need to choose where the logs (the target bucket) should be stored. The access logs may be placed in the same bucket or in another bucket. In any case, it is optional (but for good practice) to provide a prefix such as logs / or yourbucketname / logs / which will make it easier to identify your logs.

When enabled, logs are delivered with a slight delay at best. The logs contain information such as:

- Applicant account and IP address
- Bucket name
- Ask for time
- Response status or error code
- Action (GET, PUT, LIST, etc.)

Event Notifications

In response to actions taken on items uploaded or stored on Amazon S3, Amazon S3 event notifications may be sent. In response to changes made to the objects stored on Amazon S3, event notifications allow you to run workflows, submit warnings, or take other actions. You can use Amazon S3 event alerts to configure triggers to perform actions when they are downloaded, such as transcoding media files, processing data files when available, and synchronizing objects related to Amazon S3 with other data stores.

Amazon S3 event notifications are configured at the bucket level, and it can be configured through the Amazon S3 console, through the REST API, or using an AWS SDK. Amazon S3 can post notifications when new objects are created (by a PUT, POST, COPY, or multipart upload completion), when objects are deleted (by a DELETE), or when Amazon S3 detects that an RRS object was lost. You can also configure event notifications based on prefixes and suffixes of object names. Notification messages can be sent via Amazon Simple Notification Service (Amazon SNS) or Amazon Simple Queue Service (Amazon SQS) or directly to AWS Lambda to invoke AWS Lambda functions.

Best Practices, Models And Performance

It is common to use Amazon S3 storage in hybrid computing environments and applications. For example, data from local file systems, databases and compliance archives can be easily backed up over the Internet to Amazon Glacier or Amazon S3, while the main application or database storage remains on-premise.

Another common model involves using Amazon S3 as a bulk "blob" storage for data, while an index of that data is maintained in another service, such as Amazon DynamoDB or Amazon RDS. This allows for quick and complex searches for key names without constantly listing the keys.

Amazon S3 automatically scales to support very fast request rates, automatically repartitioning your buckets as needed. See the Amazon S3 best practice guidelines in the Developer Guide if you need request rates in excess of 100 requests per second. In addition, it is better to maintain a degree of random key distribution, for example, by using a hash as a prefix for key names, to support higher request rates.

Suppose you're running Amazon S3 in a GET-intensive mode, such as static website hosting, for the best performance. In this case, you should consider using an Amazon CloudFront distribution as the caching tier for your Amazon S3 bucket.

Archives

Data is kept in the archives of the Amazon Glacier. An archive can contain up to 40 TB of data, and you can possess an infinite number of archives. Upon creation, every archive is assigned a unique archive ID (You can't define a descriptive archive name, unlike an Amazon S3 object key).

Vaults

Containers for libraries are known as chests. There can be up to 1000 vaults in each AWS account. By using IAM policies or vault access policies, you can monitor access to your vaults and the actions that are permitted.

Vault Locks

You can easily implement and enforce compliance checks for individual Amazon Glacier vaults with a vault lockout policy. You can make specification controls such as Write Once Read Many (WORM) in a vault lockout policy and lock such policy against future changes. Once locked, the policy cannot be changed.

Data Recovery

You can get up to 5% of your data stored in Amazon Glacier daily for free every month. If you recover more than 5%, you will have to pay a recovery fee based on your maximum recovery rate. To eliminate or minimize these costs, you can set a data recovery policy for a vault to limit your recovery actions to free tier or to a certain data rate.

Amazon Glacier and Amazon Simple Storage Service (Amazon S3)

Amazon Glacier is similar to Amazon S3 but differs in several important aspects. Amazon Glacier supports archives of 40 TB versus objects of 5 TB in Amazon S3. Amazon Glacier archives are identified by system-generated archive IDs, Although Amazon S3 allows you use key names that are "secure". The Amazon Glacier archives are automatically encrypted, while the rest of the encryption is optional for Amazon S3. However, by using Amazon Glacier as an Amazon S3 storage class with object lifecycle policy, you can use the Amazon S3 interface to take full advantage of Amazon Glacier's benefits without learning a new interface.

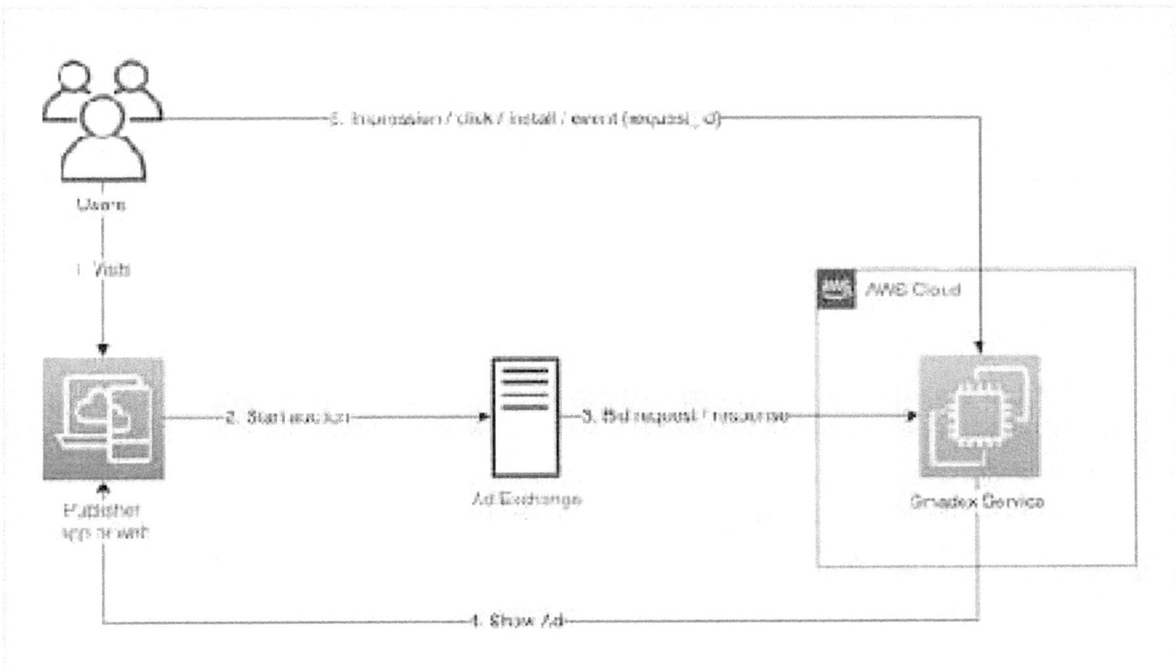

Amazon S3 is the primary object storage service on AWS and it allows you to store an unlimited amount of data with very high durability.

Common usage cases for Amazon S3 include backup and archiving, web content, big data analytics, static website hosting, hosting of mobile and cloud-native applications, and disaster recovery.

Other AWS cloud services, including AWS IAM, Amazon EBS, AWS KMS, Amazon EC2, Amazon EMR, Amazon DynamoDB, Amazon Redshift, Amazon SQS, AWS Lambda, and Amazon CloudFront, are integrated into Amazon S3.

Object storage differs from the traditional block and file storage. Block storage manages device-level data as addressable blocks, while file storage manages OS-level data in the form of files and folders.

Object storage handles data as objects that are accessible by an API, containing both data and metadata.

The Amazon S3 buckets are containers used for storing items in the Amazon S3. Globally, bucket names are often unique. Each bucket is generated in a specific region and, unless the user directly copies it, the data does not leave the region.

Pre-signed URLs enable time-limited permission to download objects and can be used against illegal "site scraping" to protect media and/or other web content.

Multipart Upload is used to upload large items, and portions of an Amazon S3 or Amazon Glacier archive can be uploaded with Range GETs.

Server access logs can be bucket enabled to track requester, subject, action, and response.

When an object is generated or removed, Amazon S3 event notifications may be used to send an Amazon SQS or Amazon SNS message or trigger an AWS Lambda function.

In Amazon S3, Amazon Glacier can be used as a standalone service or a storage class.

Exam Essentials

- Understand what Amazon s3 is and what it is commonly used for. Amazon S3 is a secure, durable and highly scalable cloud storage that can be used to store unlimited amounts of data in almost any format using a simple web services interface. Common usage cases include backup and archiving, content storage and distribution, big data analytics, static hosting of websites, cloud hosting of native software, and disaster recovery.

- Understand how storing objects varies from storing blocks and data. Object storage in the Amazon S3 cloud manages application-level data as objects using a HTTP-based REST API. Block Storage manages OS-level data in numbered addressable blocks using protocols such as SCSI or Fiber Channel. Disk storage handles data using protocols such as CIFS or NFS as OS-level shared files.
- Understand the Amazon S3 basics. Amazon S3 stores data in data and metadata-containing objects. A user-defined key identifies objects and is stored in a simple flat folder called a compartment. Native REST interfaces, multi-language SDKs, and AWS CLI and an AWS Management Console are included in the interfaces.
- Know how to create a bucket; how to upload, download, and remove objects; how to make public objects; and how to open the URL of an object.
- Understand the Amazon S3 model of data durability, availability and consistency. Amazon S3 Standard Storage is designed to last 11 nine and four nine objects in one year. The other storage classes differ. In the end, Amazon S3 is stable but provides new artifacts with read-after-write compatibility for PUTs.
- Know how to enable Amazon S3 for hosting static websites. On Amazon S3, you need to create a bucket with the website hostname to construct a static website, upload your static content and make it public, allow static website hosting on the bucket, and define index and error page objects.
- On Amazon S3, learn how to protect your data. Encrypt data with HTTPS on-the-fly and with SSE or client-side encryption at rest. Enable versions to hold different versions of an object in the bucket.
- In order to protect against accidental deletion, allow MFA Delete, using the ACL bucket policy for Amazon S3 and the access control policy for AWS IAM. For temporary download access, use pre-signed URLs. To copy data automatically to another region, use replication between regions.
- Be familiar with the usage case for each of the storage classes for Amazon S3. Data requiring high reliability, high performance, and low latency access are commonly used for general purposes. Standard-IA is available for uncommonly used data, but when accessed, it demands the same performance and availability. For easily replicable data, RRS offers lower durability at a lower cost. When the recovery time of three to five hours is appropriate, Amazon Glacier makes it possible to store infrequently used archive data at a lower cost.
- Know how to use configuration laws for the lifecycle. You can configure lifecycle rules in the AWS Management Console or in the APIs. Lifecycle configuration rules define actions for transfering objects from one storage class to another over time.
- Know how to use event alerts from Amazon S3. Event notifications are sent at the bucket level and can trigger an Amazon SNS or Amazon SQS message or an AWS Lambda action in response to an object's upload or delete.

- As a standalone operation, you know the basics of the Amazon Glacier. Data is stored in encrypted archives that can be as wide as 40 TB. Usually, archives contain TAR or ZIP files. Vaults are archive containers, and for compliance, vaults may be closed.

Review Questions

1. You need a low-latency platform where you can store files to be mounted within multiple VPC-based instances. Which of the following AWS services is the best choice?

A. AWS Storage Gateway

B. AWS S3

C. Amazon Elastic File System

D. AWS Elastic Block Store

2. What is the maximum size of S3 object metadata?

A. 2 KB

B. 5 GB

C. 100 MB

D. 5 TB

3. When planning your data operations, it's important to understand the practical limitations you'll encounter. Which of the following will be available only in limited amounts?

A. PUT requests/month against an S3 bucket

B. The volume of data available per S3 bucket

C. Account-wide S3 storage space

D. The number of S3 buckets within a single account

4. You have a publicly available file called filename, stored in an S3 bucket named bucket name. Which of the following addresses will successfully retrieve the file using a web browser?

A. https://s3.amazonaws.com/bucketname/filename

B. https://filename/bucketname.s3.amazonaws.com

C. s3://bucketname/filename

D. s3://filename/bucketname

5. If you want the files stored in an S3 bucket to be accessible using a familiar directory hierarchy system, you'll need to specify prefixes and delimiters. What are prefixes and delimiters?

A. A prefix is the name common to the objects you want to group, and a delimiter is the bar character (|).

B. A prefix is the DNS name that precedes the amazonaws.com domain, and a delimiter is the name you want to give your file directory.

C. A prefix is the name common to the objects you want to group, and a delimiter is a forward slash character (/).

D. A prefix is the name common to the file type you want to identify, and a delimiter is a forward slash character (/).

6. You want to encrypt the objects at rest in an S3 bucket using keys provided by AWS that also allows you to track related events. Which combination of tools would you use?

A. Server-side encryption with AWS KMS-Managed Keys

B. Service-side encryption with Amazon S3-Managed Keys

C. Client-side encryption with AWS KMS-Managed Keys

D. Client-side encryption with Amazon S3-Managed Keys

7. Which of the following operational details are likely to be included in S3-generated logs? (Choose three.)

A. Source bucket name

B. Action requested

C. Current bucket size

D. Response status

8. The S3 data durability guarantees cover which of the following possible threats?

(Choose two.)

A. User misconfiguration

B. Account security breach

C. Infrastructural failure

D. Data center security breach

9. Which of these explains the difference in durability between S3's S3 One Zone-IA and Reduced Redundancy classes?

A. One Zone-IA is heavily replicated but only within a single availability zone, while reduced redundancy is only lightly replicated.

B. Reduced redundancy is heavily replicated but only within a single availability zone, while One Zone-IA is only lightly replicated.

C. One Zone-IA is replicated across AWS regions, while reduced redundancy data is restricted to a single region.

D. One Zone-IA data is automatically backed up to Amazon Glacier while reduced redundancy remains within S3.

10. Which of the following is the 12-month availability guarantee for the S3 Standard-IA class?

A. 99.99 per cent

B. 99.9 per cent

C. 99.999999999 per cent

D. 99.5 percent

11. For which of the following data operations would you not worry about eventual consistency?

A. Operations immediately preceding the deletion of an existing object

B. Operations subsequent to updating of an existing object

C. Operations subsequent to the deletion of an existing object

D. Operations subsequent to the creation of a new object

12. What must you do to protect objects in S3 buckets from being accidentally overwritten?

A. Nothing. S3 protects existing files by default.

B. Nothing. S3 saves older versions of your files by default.

C. Enable versioning.

D. Enable file overwrite protection.

13. How can you apply transitions between storage classes for certain objects within an S3 bucket?

A. By specifying particular prefixes when you define your lifecycle rules

B. This isn't possible. Lifecycle rules must apply to all the objects in a bucket.

C. By specifying particular prefixes when you create the bucket

D. By importing a predefined lifecycle rule template

14. Which of the following classes will make the most sense for long-term storage when included within a sequence of lifecycle rules?

A. Glacier

B. Reduced Redundancy

C. S3 One Zone-IA

D. S3 Standard-IA

15. Which of the following are the recommended methods for providing secured and controlled access to your buckets? (Choose two.)

A. S3 access control lists (ACLs)

B. S3 bucket policies

C. IAM policies

D. Security groups

Answer to Review Questions

1. C. S3 can be used to share files, but it doesn't offer low-latency access—and its eventual consistency will not work well with file systems. Storage Gateway is designed to simplify backing up archives to the AWS cloud; it's not meant for sharing files. EBS volumes can only be used for a single instance at a time.

2. A. Object metadata contains information used by S3 to manage an object's security profile, behaviour, and the manner in which it is exposed to client requests. Storing this information requires very little space—2 KB is normally more than enough.

3. D. In theory, at least, there's no limit to the data you can upload to a single bucket or to all the buckets in your account or to the number of times you upload (using the PUT command). By default, however, you are allowed only 100 S3 buckets per account.

4. A. HTTP (web) requests must address the s3.amazon.aws.com domain along with the bucket and filenames.

5. C. A The prefix is a name common to objects that you want to group, and it is possible to use a slash character (/) as a delimiter. The bar character) (will be viewed not as a delimiter, but as part of the name.While DNS names can have prefixes, they're not relevant to S3 naming.

6. A. Client-side encryption addresses encryption before an object reaches the bucket (i.e., before it rests). Only AWS KMS-Managed Keys provide an audit trail.

7. A, B, D. Since there is no limit to the size of an S3 bucket, there would be little to gain by reporting its current size.

8. C, D. The S3 guarantee only covers the physical infrastructure owned by AWS.

9. A. One Zone-IA can be heavily replicated but only within a single availability zone, while reduced redundancy is only lightly replicated.

10. B. The S3 Standard-IA (Infrequent Access) class is guaranteed to be available 99.9 per cent of the time.

11. D. S3 can't guarantee instant consistency across their infrastructure for changes made to existing objects, but there aren't such concerns for newly created objects.

12. C. Object versioning must be manually enabled for each bucket before older versions of objects will be saved.

13. A. S3 lifecycle rules can incorporate specifying objects by the prefix. There's no such thing as a lifecycle template.

14. A. Glacier offers the least expensive and most resilient storage within the AWS ecosystem. Reduced Redundancy is not resilient, and same apply to S3 One Zone and S3 Standard.

15. B, C. ACLs is a legacy feature that isn't as flexible as IAM or S3 bucket policies. Security groups are not used equally with S3 buckets.

4. Design Resilient Architectures

Questions 1-30

Question 1.

At Examsdigest.com we use machine learning technologies to collect and analyze data, and we use Amazon Redshift for a data warehouse. Now, we need your knowledge to help us implement a disaster recovery plan for Examsdigest.com to automatically back up our cluster to a second AWS region in the event of an AWS region outage. Which of the following option will you suggest to implement?

(A) Use Amazon Redshift enhanced VPC routing

(B) Configure cross-Region snapshot

(C) Enable automated snapshots

(D) You don't need to back up the cluster to a second AWS region as Amazon Redshift is highly available

Question 2.

Which of the following Container AWS services helps you to run, stop, and manage Docker containers on a cluster?

(A) Amazon ECR

(B) Amazon ECS

(C) Amazon EKS

(D) Amazon EC2

Question 3.

Assuming you are working for a company in the gaming APP industry. The demand for your applications is growing but the performance of your APPs decreases drastically. You have been tasked to improve the performance by integrating an in-memory data store to your applications using ElastiCache. How does Amazon ElastiCache improve database performance?

(A) Cache query results and then you can quickly retrieve the data multiple times without having to re-execute the query

(B) Deliver data, videos, applications, and APIs to customers globally with low latency, high transfer speeds, all within a developer-friendly environment

(C) Reduce the load on your source DB instance by routing read queries from your applications to the read replica

(D) Enable you to build queries that efficiently navigate highly connected datasets

Question 4.

Which of the following VPC features copies the network traffic from an elastic network interface of an Amazon EC2 instance and send the traffic to monitoring appliances?

(A) Flow logs

(B) Traffic mirroring

(C) Network access control lists (ACLs)

(D) Security groups

Question 5.

There is a real-time data analytics application called DataAnalytics APP that uses AWS Lambda to process data and store the results in JSON format to an S3 bucket. In order to speed up the workflow, you have to use a service where you can run sophisticated Big Data analytics on your data without moving them into a separate analytics system. Which of the following services will you use to meet the above requirement? (Choose three answers)

(A) Amazon Redshift Spectrum

(B) DynamoDB

(C) S3 Select

(D) Amazon Athena

(E) Amazon Neptune

Question 6.

Which of the following VPC features acts as a firewall for associated subnets, controlling both inbound and outbound traffic at the subnet level?

(A) Flow logs

(B) Traffic mirroring

(C) Network access control lists (ACLs)

(D) Security groups

Question 7.

Which of the following VPC features captures information about the IP traffic going to and from network interfaces?

(A) Flow logs

(B) Traffic mirroring

(C) Network access control lists (ACLs)

(D) Security groups

Question 8.

Which of the following VPC features acts as a firewall for associated Amazon EC2 instances, controlling both inbound and outbound traffic at the instance level?

(A) Flow logs

(B) Traffic mirroring

(C) Network access control lists (ACLs)

(D) Security groups

Question 9.

You must specifically create a network path between your cluster's VPC and your data resources otherwise COPY and UNLOAD commands might fail if the VPC is not configured correctly

(A) TRUE

(B) FALSE

Question 10.

You are working as a site reliability engineer (SRE) for a large US-based IT company. You have been tasked to find an automated way to monitor and resolve issues with their on-demand EC2 instances. Which of the following option can be used to automatically monitor the EC2 instances and notify you for any possible incidents?

(A) AWS CloudFormation

(B) AWS CloudTrail

(C) Amazon CloudWatch

(D) AWS Compute Optimizer

Question 11.

You have been tasked to improve the security of the data flow between your Amazon Redshift cluster and other resources. The very first step is to use VPC flow logs to monitor all the COPY and UNLOAD traffic of your Redshift cluster that moves in and out of your VPC. Which of the following option is the most suitable solution to improve the security of your data?

(A) Enable Enhanced VPC routing on your Amazon Redshift cluster

(B) Query data with federated queries in Amazon Redshift

(C) Configure workload management

(D) Use the Amazon Redshift Spectrum

Question 12.

As a Solutions Architect for a startup, you have been tasked to provide the most suitable database service for the company in order to:

1. Store and retrieve any amount of data and serve any level of request traffic.

2. Scale up or scale down your tables' throughput capacity without downtime or performance degradation.

3. Create full backups of your tables for long-term retention and archival for regulatory compliance needs.

Which of the following Amazon database service is the most suitable solution to use to achieve the above requirements?

(A) Amazon Keyspaces

(B) Amazon Neptune

(C) Amazon DocumentDB

(D) Amazon DynamoDB

Question 13.

Which of the following Amazon Database services is compatible with MongoDB?

(A) DocumentDB

(B) Amazon Neptune

(C) Amazon Aurora

(D) Amazon RDS

Question 14.

Which of the following ACL rules allows inbound HTTP traffic from any IPv4 address.

(A) Rule: 100, Type: HTTP, Protocol: TCP, Port range: 80, Source: 0.0.0.0/0, Allow/Deny: ALLOW

(B) Rule: 100, Type: HTTP, Protocol: TCP, Port range: 443, Source: 0.0.0.0/0, Allow/Deny: ALLOW

(C) Rule: 100, Type: HTTP, Protocol: TCP, Port range: 53, Source: 0.0.0.0/0, Allow/Deny: ALLOW

(D) Rule: 100, Type: HTTP, Protocol: TCP, Port range: 22, Source: 0.0.0.0/0, Allow/Deny: ALLOW

Question 15.

Amazon ______________________ is a highly available, durable, secure, fully managed pub/sub messaging service that enables you to decouple microservices, distributed systems, and serverless applications.

(A) SQS

(B) SNS

(C) MQ

(D) SWF

Question 16.

Which of the following AWS analytic services is server less and makes it easy to analyze data in Amazon S3 using standard SQL?

(A) Amazon Athena

(B) Amazon Kinesis

(C) Amazon CloudSearch

(D) AWS Data Pipeline

Question 17.

Which of the following AWS analytic services collect, process, and analyze real-time, streaming data so you can get timely insights and react quickly to new information?

(A) Amazon Athena

(B) Amazon Kinesis

(C) Amazon CloudSearch

(D) AWS Data Pipeline

Question 18.

Which of the following AWS services is a web service that helps you reliably process and move data between different AWS compute and storage services?

(A) Amazon Athena

(B) Amazon Kinesis

(C) Amazon CloudSearch

(D) AWS Data Pipeline

Question 19.

Which of the following AWS services makes simple and cost-effective to set up, manage, and scale a search solution for your website or application?

(A) Amazon Athena

(B) Amazon Kinesis

(C) Amazon CloudSearch

(D) AWS Data Pipeline

Question 20.

You can use Amazon ________________ Logs to monitor, store, and access your log files from Amazon Elastic Compute Cloud (Amazon EC2) instances, AWS CloudTrail, Route 53, and other sources.

(A) CloudWatch

(B) CloudTrail

(C) Lambda

(D) CloudMonitor

Question 21.

Your company has a VPC for the IT department, and other VPC for the accounting department. Which type of networking connection in AWS should you use for the IT department in order to get access to all resources that are in the accounting department, and vice versa?

(A) VPC peering

(B) ClassicLink

(C) Elastic IP addresses

(D) VPC endpoints

Question 22.

You have just launched an EC2 instance in a subnet into your VPC. After investigation, you have realized that the EC2 instance isn't accessible from the Internet. What could be the primary cause of this issue?

(A) The route table is not configured properly

(B) The DNS hostname is wrong

(C) The VPC is not enabled for ClassicLink

(D) VPC peering connection is not created

Question 23.

A social media application that collects, processes, and analyzes feed data in real-time is using Kinesis Data Streams. What service will you use to send stream records directly to services such as Amazon Simple Storage Service (Amazon S3) or Amazon Redshift instead of creating a consumer application?

(A) Amazon Kinesis Data Firehose

(B) Amazon QuickSight

(C) Amazon Athena

(D) Amazon AppFlow

Question 24.

An EC2 instance ___________________ provides temporary block-level storage for your instance and is ideal for the temporary storage of information that changes frequently, such as buffers, caches, scratch data.

(A) Store

(B) Cache

(C) Data

(D) Block

Question 25.

You are working as a Solutions Architect for a service marketplace startup. A tech stack includes MariaDB. You have been tasked to migrate the database to AWS to improve the performance and make the DB highly available in case of database server failure in the future. Which of the following option is the best way to meet the requirement?

(A) Create a MariaDB database in RDS with Multi-AZ deployments

(B) Create a MariaDB database in Amazon Aurora

(C) Create a Redshift

(D) Create a DynamoDB

Question 26.

Which of the following function setting requires adjustment in order to allow a Lamba function to run for 900 seconds before stopping the execution?

(A) Memory

(B) Timeout

(C) Concurrency

(D) Handler

Question 27.

It is considered as a best practice to rely on instance store for valuable, long-term data, instead of using Amazon S3, Amazon EBS, or Amazon EFS.

(A) TRUE

(B) FALSE

Question 28.

You are an AWS consultant for a company that currently has an on-premises infrastructure and they have a plan to extend their storage capacity using AWS services. Which AWS service can help the company to achieve this requirement?

(A) AWS Storage Gateway

(B) AWS Snow Family

(C) Amazon Elastic Block Store

(D) Amazon Elastic File System

Question 29.

You have recently launched an EC2 instance that is hosting your new web application. The volume of users is expected to grow in the coming days as you are planning to post the product on producthunt.com. What AWS services will you use in order to handle the demand and keep the users satisfied? (Choose two answers)

(A) Use AWS Global Accelerator

(B) Set up two EC2 instances and create an Elastic Load Balancer

(C) Enable AWS Shield Standard

(D) Set up an Amazon GuardDuty

Question 30.

You are working for an eCommerce startup as a Solutions Architect. You have been tasked to implement a solution so each time the inventory of a specific product collection reaches the out-of-stock level to get notified instantly. Which AWS service will you use to accomplish this requirement?

(A) Amazon Stock Notification Service

(B) Amazon Product Notification Service

(C) Amazon Simple Notification Service

(D) Amazon Inventory Notification Service

Answers 1-30

Question 1.

At Examsdigest.com we use machine learning technologies to collect and analyze data, and we use Amazon Redshift for a data warehouse. Now, we need your knowledge to help us implement a disaster recovery plan for Examsdigest.com to automatically back up our cluster to a second AWS region in the event of an AWS region outage. Which of the following option will you suggest to implement?

(A) Use Amazon Redshift enhanced VPC routing

(B) Configure cross-Region snapshot

(C) Enable automated snapshots

(D) You don't need to back up the cluster to a second AWS region as Amazon Redshift is highly available

Explanation 1.

Configure cross-Region snapshot is the correct answer.

You can configure Amazon Redshift to copy snapshots for a cluster to another AWS Region. To configure cross-Region snapshot copy, you need to enable this copy feature for each cluster and configure where to copy snapshots and how long to keep copied automated snapshots in the destination AWS Region. When cross-Region copy is enabled for a cluster, all new manual and automated snapshots are copied to the specified AWS Region. Copied snapshot names are prefixed with copy:.

Question 2.

Which of the following Container AWS services helps you to run, stop, and manage Docker containers on a cluster?

(A) Amazon ECR

(B) Amazon ECS

(C) Amazon EKS

(D) Amazon EC2

Explanation 2.

Amazon ECS is the correct answer.

Amazon Elastic Container Service (Amazon ECS) is a highly scalable, fast, container management service that helps to run, stop, and manage Docker containers on a cluster.

You can host your cluster on a serverless infrastructure that is managed by Amazon ECS by launching your services or tasks using the Fargate launch type. For more control over your infrastructure, you can host your tasks on a cluster of Amazon Elastic Compute Cloud (Amazon EC2) instances that you manage by using the EC2 launch type.

Question 3.

Assuming you are working for a company in the gaming APP industry. The demand for your applications is growing but the performance of your APPs decreases drastically. You have been tasked to improve the performance by integrating an in-memory data store to your applications using ElastiCache. How does Amazon ElastiCache improve database performance?

(A) Cache query results and then you can quickly retrieve the data multiple times without having to re-execute the query

(B) Deliver data, videos, applications, and APIs to customers globally with low latency, high transfer speeds, all within a developer-friendly environment

(C) Reduce the load on your source DB instance by routing read queries from your applications to the read replica

(D) Enable you to build queries that efficiently navigate highly connected datasets

Explanation 3.

Cache query results and then you can quickly retrieve the data multiple times without having to re-execute the query is the correct answer.

Amazon ElastiCache allows you to seamlessly set up, run, and scale popular open-Source compatible in-memory data stores in the cloud. Build data-intensive apps or boost the performance of

your existing databases by retrieving data from high throughput and low latency in-memory data stores.

Amazon ElastiCache is a popular choice for real-time use cases like Caching, Session Stores, Gaming, Geospatial Services, Real-Time Analytics, and Queuing.

The primary purpose of an in-memory key-value store is to provide ultrafast (submillisecond latency) and inexpensive access to copies of data.

Question 4.

Which of the following VPC features copies the network traffic from an elastic network interface of an Amazon EC2 instance and send the traffic to monitoring appliances?

(A) Flow logs

(B) Traffic mirroring

(C) Network access control lists (ACLs)

(D) Security groups

Explanation 4.

Traffic mirroring is the correct answer.

Traffic mirroring copies network traffic from an elastic network interface of an Amazon EC2 instance and then you can then send the traffic to out-of-band security and monitoring appliances.

Question 5.

There is a real-time data analytics application called DataAnalytics APP that uses AWS Lambda to process data and store the results in JSON format to an S3 bucket. In order to speed up the workflow, you have to use a service where you can run sophisticated Big Data analytics on your data without moving them into a separate analytics system. Which of the following services will you use to meet the above requirement? (Choose three answers)

(A) Amazon Redshift Spectrum

(B) DynamoDB

(C) S3 Select

(D) Amazon Athena

(E) Amazon Neptune

Explanation 5.

The services will you use to meet the above requirement are Amazon Redshift Spectrum, S3 Select, Amazon Athena.

Amazon Redshift Spectrum

– is a feature within Amazon Web Services' Redshift data warehousing service that lets a data analyst conduct fast, complex analysis on objects stored on the AWS cloud.

S3 Select

– is designed to pull out only the data you need from an object, which can dramatically improve the performance and reduce the cost of applications that need to access data in S3.

Amazon Athena

– is an interactive query service that makes it easy to analyze data in Amazon S3 using standard SQL. Athena is serverless, so there is no infrastructure to manage, and you pay only for the queries that you run.

Question 6.

Which of the following VPC features acts as a firewall for associated subnets, controlling both inbound and outbound traffic at the subnet level?

(A)

Flow logs

(B) Traffic mirroring

(C) Network access control lists (ACLs)

(D) Security groups

Explanation 6.

Network access control lists (ACLs) is the correct answer.

Network ACLs act as a firewall for associated subnets, controlling both inbound and outbound traffic at the subnet level.

Question 7.

Which of the following VPC features captures information about the IP traffic going to and from network interfaces?

(A) Flow logs

(B) Traffic mirroring

(C) Network access control lists (ACLs)

(D) Security groups

Explanation 7.

Flow logs is the correct answer.

Flow logs capture information about the IP traffic going to and from network interfaces in your VPC. You can create a flow log for a VPC, subnet, or individual network interface. Flow log data is published to CloudWatch Logs or Amazon S3, and it can help you diagnose overly restrictive or overly permissive security groups and network ACL rules.

Question 8.

Which of the following VPC features acts as a firewall for associated Amazon EC2 instances, controlling both inbound and outbound traffic at the instance level?

(A) Flow logs

(B) Traffic mirroring

(C) Network access control lists (ACLs)

(D) Security groups

Explanation 8.

Security groups is the correct answer.

Security groups act as a firewall for associated Amazon EC2 instances, controlling both inbound and outbound traffic at the instance level. When you launch an instance, you can associate it with one or more security groups that you've created. Each instance in your VPC could belong to a different set of security groups. If you don't specify a security group when you launch an instance, the instance is automatically associated with the default security group for the VPC.

Question 9.

You must specifically create a network path between your cluster's VPC and your data resources otherwise COPY and UNLOAD commands might fail if the VPC is not configured correctly

(A) TRUE

(B) FALSE

Explanation 9.

TRUE is the correct answer.

Because enhanced VPC routing affects the way that Amazon Redshift accesses other resources, COPY and UNLOAD commands might fail unless you configure your VPC correctly. You must specifically create a network path between your cluster's VPC and your data resources.

Question 10.

You are working as a site reliability engineer (SRE) for a large US-based IT company. You have been tasked to find an automated way to monitor and resolve issues with their on-demand EC2 instances. Which of the following option can be used to automatically monitor the EC2 instances and notify you for any possible incidents?

(A) AWS CloudFormation

(B) AWS CloudTrail

(C) Amazon CloudWatch

(D) AWS Compute Optimizer

Explanation 10.

Amazon CloudWatch is the correct answer.

CloudWatch provides you with data and actionable insights to monitor your applications, respond to system-wide performance changes, optimize resource utilization, and get a unified view of operational health.

CloudWatch collects monitoring and operational data in the form of logs and events, providing you with a unified view of AWS resources, and services that run on AWS and on-premises servers.

You can use CloudWatch to detect anomalous behavior in your environments, set alarms, visualize logs and metrics side by side, take automated actions, troubleshoot issues, and discover insights to keep your applications running smoothly.

Question 11.

You have been tasked to improve the security of the data flow between your Amazon Redshift cluster and other resources. The very first step is to use VPC flow logs to monitor all the COPY and UNLOAD traffic of your Redshift cluster that moves in and out of your VPC. Which of the following option is the most suitable solution to improve the security of your data?

(A) Enable Enhanced VPC routing on your Amazon Redshift cluster

(B) Query data with federated queries in Amazon Redshift

(C) Configure workload management

(D) Use the Amazon Redshift Spectrum

Explanation 11.

Enable Enhanced VPC routing on your Amazon Redshift cluster is the correct answer.

When you use Amazon Redshift enhanced VPC routing, Amazon Redshift forces all COPY and UNLOAD traffic between your cluster and your data repositories through your Amazon VPC. By using enhanced VPC routing, you can use standard VPC features, such as VPC security groups, network access control lists (ACLs), VPC endpoints, VPC endpoint policies, internet gateways, and Domain Name System (DNS) servers. You use these features to tightly manage the flow of data between your Amazon Redshift cluster and other resources.

When you use enhanced VPC routing to route traffic through your VPC, you can also use VPC flow logs to monitor COPY and UNLOAD traffic.

If enhanced VPC routing is not enabled, Amazon Redshift routes traffic through the internet, including traffic to other services within the AWS network.

Question 12.

As a Solutions Architect for a startup, you have been tasked to provide the most suitable database service for the company in order to:

1. Store and retrieve any amount of data and serve any level of request traffic.

2. Scale up or scale down your tables' throughput capacity without downtime or performance degradation.

3. Create full backups of your tables for long-term retention and archival for regulatory compliance needs.

Which of the following Amazon database service is the most suitable solution to use to achieve the above requirements?

(A) Amazon Keyspaces

(B) Amazon Neptune

(C) Amazon DocumentDB

(D) Amazon DynamoDB

Explanation 12.

Amazon DynamoDB is the correct answer.

Amazon DynamoDB is a fully managed NoSQL database service that provides fast and predictable performance with seamless scalability.

With DynamoDB:

1) You can create database tables that can store and retrieve any amount of data and serve any level of request traffic.

2) You can scale up or scale down your tables' throughput capacity without downtime or performance degradation.

3) You can create full backups of your tables for long-term retention and archival for regulatory compliance needs.

4) You can enable point-in-time recovery for your Amazon DynamoDB tables.

5) You can delete expired items from tables automatically to help you reduce storage usage and the cost of storing data that is no longer relevant.

Question 13.

Which of the following Amazon Database services is compatible with MongoDB?

(A) DocumentDB

(B) Amazon Neptune

(C) Amazon Aurora

(D) Amazon RDS

Explanation 13.

DocumentDB is the correct answer.

Amazon DocumentDB is compatible with MongoDB, is a fast, reliable, and fully-managed database service. Amazon DocumentDB makes it easy to set up, operate, and scale MongoDB-compatible databases in the cloud. With Amazon DocumentDB, you can run the same application code and use the same drivers and tools that you use with MongoDB.

Question 14.

Which of the following ACL rules allows inbound HTTP traffic from any IPv4 address.

(A) Rule: 100, Type: HTTP, Protocol: TCP, Port range: 80, Source: 0.0.0.0/0, Allow/Deny: ALLOW

(B) Rule: 100, Type: HTTP, Protocol: TCP, Port range: 443, Source: 0.0.0.0/0, Allow/Deny: ALLOW

(C) Rule: 100, Type: HTTP, Protocol: TCP, Port range: 53, Source: 0.0.0.0/0, Allow/Deny: ALLOW

(D) Rule: 100, Type: HTTP, Protocol: TCP, Port range: 22, Source: 0.0.0.0/0, Allow/Deny: ALLOW

Explanation 14.

Rule: 100, Type: HTTP, Protocol: TCP, Port range: 80, Source: 0.0.0.0/0, Allow/Deny: ALLOW is the correct answer.

1)

Rule: 100, Type: HTTP, Protocol: TCP, Port range: 443, Source: 0.0.0.0/0, Allow/Deny: ALLOW is incorrect because it uses the port 443 which is the HTTPS port

2)

Rule: 100, Type: HTTP, Protocol: TCP, Port range: 53, Source: 0.0.0.0/0, Allow/Deny: ALLOW is incorrect because it uses the port 53 which is the DNS port

3)

Rule: 100, Type: HTTP, Protocol: TCP, Port range: 22, Source: 0.0.0.0/0, Allow/Deny: ALLOW is incorrect because it uses the port 22 which is the SSH port

Question 15.

Amazon ________________________ is a highly available, durable, secure, fully managed pub/sub messaging service that enables you to decouple microservices, distributed systems, and serverless applications.

(A) SQS

(B) SNS

(C) MQ

(D) SWF

Explanation 15.

SNS is the correct answer.

Amazon Simple Notification Service (SNS) is a highly available, durable, secure, fully managed pub/sub messaging service that enables you to decouple microservices, distributed systems, and serverless applications.

Amazon SNS provides topics for high-throughput, push-based, many-to-many messaging. Using Amazon SNS topics, your publisher systems can fan-out messages to a large number of subscriber endpoints for parallel processing, including Amazon SQS queues, AWS Lambda functions, and HTTP/S webhooks. Additionally, SNS can be used to fan out notifications to end users using mobile push, SMS, and email.

Question 16.

Which of the following AWS analytic services is serverless and makes it easy to analyze data in Amazon S3 using standard SQL?

(A) Amazon Athena

(B) Amazon Kinesis

(C) Amazon CloudSearch

(D) AWS Data Pipeline

Explanation 16.

Amazon Athena is the correct answer.

Amazon Athena is an interactive query service that makes it easy to analyze data in Amazon S3 using standard SQL. Athena is serverless, so there is no infrastructure to manage, and you pay only for the queries that you run.

Athena is easy to use. Simply point to your data in Amazon S3, define the schema, and start querying using standard SQL.

Most results are delivered within seconds. With Athena, there's no need for complex ETL jobs to prepare your data for analysis. This makes it easy for anyone with SQL skills to quickly analyze large-scale datasets.

Question 17.

Which of the following AWS analytic services collect, process, and analyze real-time, streaming data so you can get timely insights and react quickly to new information?

(A) Amazon Athena

(B) Amazon Kinesis

(C) Amazon CloudSearch

(D) AWS Data Pipeline

Explanation 17.

Amazon Kinesis is the correct answer.

Amazon Kinesis makes it easy to collect, process, and analyze real-time, streaming data so you can get timely insights and react quickly to new information. Amazon Kinesis offers key capabilities to cost-effectively process streaming data at any scale, along with the flexibility to choose the tools that best suit the requirements of your application.

Question 18.

Which of the following AWS services is a web service that helps you reliably process and move data between different AWS compute and storage services?

(A) Amazon Athena

(B) Amazon Kinesis

(C) Amazon CloudSearch

(D) AWS Data Pipeline

Explanation 18.

AWS Data Pipeline is the correct answer.

AWS Data Pipeline is a web service that helps you reliably process and move data between different AWS compute and storage services, as well as on-premises data sources, at specified intervals.

With AWS Data Pipeline, you can access your data where it's stored, transform and process it at scale, and efficiently transfer the results to S3, Amazon RDS and Amazon EMR.

Question 19.

Which of the following AWS services makes simple and cost-effective to set up, manage, and scale a search solution for your website or application?

(A) Amazon Athena

(B) Amazon Kinesis

(C) Amazon CloudSearch

(D) AWS Data Pipeline

Explanation 19.

Amazon CloudSearch is the correct answer.

Amazon CloudSearch is a managed service in the AWS Cloud that makes it simple and cost-effective to set up, manage, and scale a search solution for your website or application.

With Amazon CloudSearch, you can quickly add rich search capabilities to your website or application. You don't need to become a search expert or worry about hardware provisioning, setup, and maintenance. With a few clicks in the AWS Management Console, you can create a search domain and upload the data that you want to make searchable, and Amazon CloudSearch will automatically provision the required resources and deploy a highly tuned search index.

Question 20.

You can use Amazon ________________ Logs to monitor, store, and access your log files from Amazon Elastic Compute Cloud (Amazon EC2) instances, AWS CloudTrail, Route 53, and other sources.

(A) CloudWatch

(B) CloudTrail

(C) Lambda

(D) CloudMonitor

Explanation 20.

Amazon CloudWatch is the correct answer.

You can use Amazon CloudWatch Logs to monitor, store, and access your log files from Amazon Elastic Compute Cloud (Amazon EC2) instances, AWS CloudTrail, Route 53, and other sources.

CloudWatch Logs enables you to centralize the logs from all of your systems, applications, and AWS services that you use, in a single, highly scalable service. You can then easily view them, search them for specific error codes or patterns, filter them

based on specific fields, or archive them securely for future analysis.

Question 21.

Your company has a VPC for the IT department, and other VPC for the accounting department. Which type of networking connection in AWS should you use for the IT department in order to get access to all resources that are in the accounting department, and vice versa?

(A) VPC peering

(B) ClassicLink

(C) Elastic IP addresses

(D) VPC endpoints

Explanation 21.

VPC peering is the correct answer.

A VPC peering connection is a networking connection between two VPCs that enables you to route traffic between them using private IPv4 addresses or IPv6 addresses.

Instances in either VPC can communicate with each other as if they are within the same network. The VPCs can be in different regions (also known as an inter-region VPC peering connection).

Question 22.

You have just launched an EC2 instance in a subnet into your VPC. After investigation, you have realized that the EC2 instance isn't accessible from the Internet. What could be the primary cause of this issue?

(A) The route table is not configured properly

(B) The DNS hostname is wrong

(C) The VPC is not enabled for ClassicLink

(D) VPC peering connection is not created

Explanation 22.

The route table is not configured properly is the correct answer.

Each route in a table specifies a destination and a target. To enable your subnet to access the internet through an internet gateway, add the following route to your subnet route table.

Destination

Target

0.0.0.0/0

igw-id

The destination for the route is 0.0.0.0/0, which represents all IPv4 addresses. The target is the internet gateway that's attached to your VPC

Question 23.

A social media application that collects, processes, and analyzes feed data in real-time is using Kinesis Data Streams. What service will you use to send stream records directly to services such as Amazon Simple Storage Service (Amazon S3) or Amazon Redshift instead of creating a consumer application?

(A) Amazon Kinesis Data Firehose

(B) Amazon QuickSight

(C) Amazon Athena

(D) Amazon AppFlow

Explanation 23.

Amazon Kinesis Data Firehose is the correct answer.

A consumer, known as an Amazon Kinesis Data Streams application, is an application that you build to read and process data records from Kinesis data streams.

If you want to send stream records directly to services such as Amazon Simple Storage Service (Amazon S3), Amazon Redshift, Amazon Elasticsearch Service (Amazon ES), or Splunk, you can use a

Kinesis Data Firehose delivery stream

instead of creating a consumer application.

Amazon Kinesis Data Firehose

is a fully managed service for delivering real-time streaming data to destinations such as Amazon S3, Amazon Redshift, Amazon Elasticsearch Service (Amazon ES), and Splunk. Kinesis Data Firehose is part of the Kinesis streaming data platform, along with Kinesis Data Streams, Kinesis Video Streams, and Amazon Kinesis Data Analytics.

With Kinesis Data Firehose, you don't need to write applications or manage resources. You configure your data producers to send data to Kinesis Data Firehose, and it automatically delivers the data to the destination that you specified.

Question 24.

An EC2 instance ____________________ provides temporary block-level storage for your instance and is ideal for the temporary storage of information that changes frequently, such as buffers, caches, scratch data.

(A) Store

(B) Cache

(C) Data

(D) Block

Explanation 24.

Store is the correct answer.

An EC2 instance store provides temporary block-level storage for your instance and is ideal for the temporary storage of information that changes frequently, such as buffers, caches, scratch data. The data in an instance store persists only during the lifetime of its associated instance.

If an instance reboots (intentionally or unintentionally), data in the instance store persists. However, data in the instance store is lost under any of the following circumstances:

1)

The underlying disk drive fails

2)

The instance stops

3)

The instance terminates

Question 25.

You are working as a Solutions Architect for a service marketplace startup. A tech stack includes MariaDB. You have been tasked to migrate the database to AWS to improve the performance and make the DB highly available in case of database server failure in the future. Which of the following option is the best way to meet the requirement?

(A) Create a MariaDB database in RDS with Multi-AZ deployments

(B) Create a MariaDB database in Amazon Aurora

(C) Create a Redshift

(D) Create a DynamoDB

Explanation 25.

Create a MariaDB database in RDS with Multi-AZ deployments is the correct answer.

Amazon RDS Multi-AZ deployments provide enhanced availability and durability for RDS database (DB) instances, making them a natural fit for production database workloads. When you provision a Multi-AZ DB Instance, Amazon RDS automatically creates a primary DB Instance and synchronously replicates the data to a standby instance in a different Availability Zone (AZ).

Multi-AZ deployments for the MySQL,

MariaDB

, Oracle, and PostgreSQL engines utilize synchronous physical replication to keep data on the standby up-to-date with the primary. If an Availability Zone failure or DB Instance failure occurs, your availability impact is limited to the time automatic failover takes to complete: typically under one minute for Amazon Aurora (as little as 30 seconds when using the MariaDB Connector/J).

Question 26.

Which of the following function setting requires adjustment in order to allow a Lamba function to run for 900 seconds before stopping the execution?

(A) Memory

(B) Timeout

(C) Concurrency

(D) Handler

Explanation 26.

Timeout is the correct answer.

AWS Lambda is a compute service that lets you run code without provisioning or managing servers. AWS Lambda executes your code only when needed and scales automatically, from a few requests per day to thousands per second.

You can use the Lambda console to configure function settings, add triggers and destinations, and update and test your code. The function setting that requires adjustment to allow a function to run for 900 seconds is

Timeout.

Timeout

is the amount of time that Lambda allows a function to run before stopping it. The default is 3 seconds. The maximum allowed value is 900 seconds.

Question 27.

It is considered as a best practice to rely on instance store for valuable, long-term data, instead of using Amazon S3, Amazon EBS, or Amazon EFS.

(A) TRUE

(B) FALSE

Explanation 27.

False is the correct answer.

The data in an instance store persists only during the lifetime of its associated instance. If an instance reboots (intentionally or unintentionally), data in the instance store persists. However, data in the instance store is lost under any of the following circumstances:

1)

The underlying disk drive fails

2)

The instance stops

3)

The instance terminates

Therefore,

is not a good practice

to rely on instance store for valuable, long-term data. Instead, use more durable data storage, such as Amazon S3, Amazon EBS, or Amazon EFS.

Question 28.

You are an AWS consultant for a company that currently has an on-premises infrastructure and they have a plan to extend their storage capacity using AWS services. Which AWS service can help the company to achieve this requirement?

(A) AWS Storage Gateway

(B) AWS Snow Family

(C) Amazon Elastic Block Store

(D) Amazon Elastic File System

Explanation 28.

AWS Storage Gateway is the correct answer.

AWS Storage Gateway connects an on-premises software appliance with cloud-based storage to provide seamless integration with data security features between your on-premises IT environment and the AWS storage infrastructure. You can use the service to store data in the AWS Cloud for scalable and cost-effective storage that helps maintain data security.

Question 29.

You have recently launched an EC2 instance that is hosting your new web application. The volume of users is expected to grow in the coming days as you are planning to post the product on producthunt.com. What AWS services will you use in order to handle the demand and keep the users satisfied? (Choose two answers)

(A) Use AWS Global Accelerator

(B) Set up two EC2 instances and create an Elastic Load Balancer

(C) Enable AWS Shield Standard

(D) Set up an Amazon GuardDuty

Explanation 29.

Use AWS Global Accelerator and Set up two EC2 instances and create an Elastic Load Balancer are the correct answers.

Global Accelerator

is a service in which you create accelerators to improve the availability and performance of your applications for local and global users.

Global Accelerator directs traffic to optimal endpoints over the AWS global network. This improves the availability and performance of your internet applications that are used by a global audience.

Elastic Load Balancing

distributes incoming application or network traffic across multiple targets, such as Amazon EC2 instances, containers, and IP addresses, in multiple Availability Zones.

Elastic Load Balancing scales your load balancer as traffic to your application changes over time. It can automatically scale to the vast majority of workloads.

Question 30.

You are working for an eCommerce startup as a Solutions Architect. You have been tasked to implement a solution so each time the inventory of a specific product collection reaches the out-of-stock level to get notified instantly. Which AWS service will you use to accomplish this requirement?

(A) Amazon Stock Notification Service

(B) Amazon Product Notification Service

(C) Amazon Simple Notification Service

(D) Amazon Inventory Notification Service

Explanation 30.

Amazon Simple Notification Service is the correct answer.

The

Amazon Simple Notification Service

can support a wide variety of needs including event notification, monitoring applications mobile applications, and any other application that generates or consumes notifications.

For example, Amazon SNS can be used in workflow systems to relay events among distributed computer applications, move data between data stores, or update records in business systems. Event updates and notifications concerning validation, approval, inventory changes, and shipment status are immediately delivered to relevant system components as well as end-users.

5. Management Tools

Numerous companies and individuals are bound by their standards or some complex regulatory commitments and are still reluctant to place their data in a cloud for the fear of loss or theft. However, this resistance is blurring, as logical isolation has demonstrated reliability. Additionally, data encryption and different characters including access management tools have improved security inside the public cloud.

AWS Management Tools

Provisioning

AWS CloudFormation is a program that features an ordinary language that you can explain and provision all of the infrastructure materials in the cloud atmosphere. CloudFormation encourages the user in utilizing documents as well as offers surveillance securely and automatically. The moment everything is modeled, this particular document is the one source of the fact of the cloud atmosphere. Inside AWS Service the person is able to generate a group of permitted CloudFormation data. Catalog to permit the organization to entirely deploy approved and compliant information.

Monitoring and Working

Amazon CloudWatch might be a seeing service for AWS cloud energy and definitely, the apps you operate—Positive Many Meanings—on AWS. The person is able to collect as well as monitor information. They could further use it to observe log data. AWS CloudWatch conjointly offers a stream of events describing changes to the AWS resources that you will work with to respond to changes in the applications.

Managed Services

OpsWorks removes the need to work with the user's configuration control methods. It conjointly works seamlessly together with your current chef as well as Puppet equipment. OpsWorks could immediately spot, update, and backup the Cook as well as Puppet servers and keep their source too. OpsWorks is a great selection if you are a current user of Puppet or Cook.

AWS Management Tools Services

These are several solutions provided by AWS Management Tools.

AWS CloudFormation

Amazon CloudFormation encourages the user to control and provides the whole infrastructure by using programming languages. AWS CloudFormation lets you utilize an easy computer system file to model and also provides, in a secure and automatic fashion, all of the materials necessary for the application, throughout all the accounts and regions. This particular file is the one source of fact for the cloud atmosphere.

AWS Service Catalog

AWS Service Catalog will help the group to handle catalogs of its services. These solutions often are utilized on AWS. These IT services will embrace virtual machine photographs, software, servers, along with directories to complete multi-tier program architectures. AWS Service Catalog offers a center through which a person can centrally manage typically deployed IT services, see the compliance needs, and also helps to attain consistent governance.

AWS Systems Manager

AWS Systems Manager provides you with management and visibility of the infrastructure on AWS. Systems Manager offers an application whereby the person is able to check functional information from multiple AWS services. Additionally, it enables the person to automate functional things across the AWS resources. Systems Manager offers an advantage whereby the person will have the ability to cluster online resources, including Amazon EC2 instances, Amazon S3 buckets, or maybe Amazon RDS cases. This may be accomplished by the application program, reading functional details for watching and also troubleshooting, and also doing something on the teams of online resources.

AWS CloudTrail

There are numerous facilities that a user receives from AWS CloudTrail, including governance, operational auditing, compliance, and chance auditing of the AWS account. This particular event simplifies troubleshooting, resource modification chase, and security analysis.

AWS Config

AWS Config might be a program that enables you to evaluate, audit, and determine the configurations of the AWS resources. With all the assistance of Configuration, one could easily check as well as document the AWS source configurations and also allows the person to automate the evaluation of recorded configurations against ideal configurations. Config additionally offers other advantages: the person is going to be ready to discuss changes in relationships and configurations between AWS online resources; he can dive into intricate source configuration histories; he can also confirm the general compliance from the configurations per the inner pointers. This enables the user to alter compliance auditing, modification management, security analysis, and functional troubleshooting.

Security, undoubtedly, is always a major concern for organizations mulling over cloud adoption, particularly for public cloud appropriation. A public cloud specialist shares its basic hardware infrastructure with various clients. However, this condition requests plentiful isolation between logical computing assets. Simultaneously, access to public cloud storage and process assets is monitored by account login accreditations.

Cloud security at AWS is the most noteworthy. As a client, you will profit by a server center and system designed to meet the necessities of the most security-delicate associations. Security in the cloud is a lot like security in your on-premises server farms, but without the expenses of keeping up offices and equipment. In the cloud, you don't need to oversee physical servers or storage gadgets. Instead, you use software-based security instruments to ensure the flow of data into and out of your cloud resources.

Questions

Question 1:

What are the two types of methods you can use to configure the authenticator app on your mobile device?

Question 2:

In your custom VPC, you launch an 'internet-facing' public load balancer with an HTTP listener on Port 80 load, balancing HTTP traffic to a pair of web servers. You have verified that the DNS resolution of the load balancer name does indeed resolve to public IP addresses. Also, you have verified the website is accessible by browsing directly to the webserver IP addresses, and both instances are registered and are in service on the load balancer. However, users on the public internet get the 'HTTP 404: Page Not Found' error when trying to access the website hosted on the ELB. What could be the cause?

a) There are no NAT instance setups in the VPC.

b) You need to assign elastic IPS to the load balancer.

c) The load balancer was created in private subnets.

d) VPC CIDR range needs to be a public IP address range.

Question 3:

Which of the following metrics are not available in basic CloudWatch monitoring? (Choose two answers)

- Memory utilization
- Network bytes out
- CPU utilization
- Disk space utilization
- Average disk queue length

Question 4:

Auto-scaling supports which of the following strategies for scaling out of instances? (Choose 3 answers).

Predictive

Scheduled

Dynamic

Manual

Optimistic

Question 5:

What are the minimum, maximum, and default message visibility timeout values for an SQS message?

a) minimum=0, maximum=12 hours, default=30 seconds

b) minimum=30 seconds, maximum=24 hours, default=300 seconds

c) minimum=0, maximum=300 seconds, default=30 seconds

d) minimum=0, maximum=12 hours, default=60 seconds

Each queue starts with a default setting of 30 seconds for the visibility timeout.

The maximum visibility timeout for a message is 12 hours.

Answers

Question 1 Answer:

You can configure MFA either using the bar code scanning option or by directly entering the authentication key.

Question 2 Answer: C

This is a frequently seen misconfiguration. Internet-facing public load balancers should be on public subnets.

Question 3 Answer: A, D

Basic CloudWatch monitoring only collects hypervisor level metrics. It does not collect OS metrics like memory and disk usage.

Question 4 Answer: B, D

Question 5 Answer: C

CloudTrail and Config together can provide details on who made the change and what changes were made.

6. Design High Performant Architectures

This chapter will cover the best practices for designing performant architectures. At the end of the chapter, there will be a set of practice test questions to give an idea of what the questions will be like in this section of the exam.

Design Performant Architectures Best Practices

The following are the best practices for designing performant AWS architectures.

Storage and Databases

Storage

When choosing storage service based on performance, you should look at solutions such as EBS with a few storage solutions to choose from.

When looking at choosing EBS as an option, one must first decide if SSD or HDD better fits the environment. Once that decision has been made it will need to be narrowed down further to choose the drive based on the required type of performance.

Another way to improve performance is by using Amazon S3 to load all static content from any web server(s). Once static content is taken off a web server, it will improve the server performance as resources will not have to be allocated to the static content. The web server is freed up to deal with dynamic content.

By creating a bucket in one of the AWS Regions, content such as videos, documents, and photos can be uploaded to Amazon S3.

You can find more information on how to upload content to Amazon S3 at the following link:

https://docs.aws.amazon.com/AmazonS3/latest/user-guide/upload-objects.html

Amazon S3 objects are assigned a URL that is based on the name of the Bucket. It should be noted that Bucket names are unique, and once a bucket name has been created, it cannot be used anywhere else in the world, similar to that of a domain name.

There are different payment structures and storage classes for Amazon S3:

- Amazon S3 Standard Access is the best for general purpose usage.

- Amazon S3 Standard Infrequent Access (IA) gives a lower cost per GB of storage but has a higher charge for GET, PUT, COPY, and POST requests. It also has a minimum 30-day storage requirement.

One of Amazon S3 best features is that lifecycle policies can be set to move files to the Amazon S3 infrequent use and eventually to a service like Glacier for archiving and eventually deleted if the data permits it.

Database

Amazon offers many database solutions such as:

- Relational database service—Using Amazon RDS
  - RDS is designed to offer a managed relational database.
  - RDS offers high durability for complex transactions or queries.
  - It can only have a single worker node.
  - It should not be used for sharding or RDBMS customization.
  - It cannot be used for read/writes that exceed 150k write per second.
  - The RDS master database can be scaled up and this can be done by using a bigger RDS instance.
  - The RDS master database can also be scaled up by using RDS Read Replicas.
    - RDS Read Replicas are supported by MySQL, Postgres, Aurora, and MariaDB
    - RDS Read Replicas work by distributing read requests to the Read Replicas which takes the load off the RDS Master database
  - You can find more information on RDs at the following links.

https://docs.aws.amazon.com/AmazonRDS/latest/UserGuide/Welcome.html

https://docs.aws.amazon.com/AmazonRDS/latest/UserGuide/CHAP_GettingStarted.html

- Managed no sequel database—Using Amazon DynamoDB
  - For high read rates or throughput DynamoDB is the best solution.
  - Scaling horizontally by adding more servers so it can offer limitless storage.

- Automatic Sharding of data and splits it across servers.
- DynamoDB uses throughput capacity requirements (read/write) to allocate resources.
- It is easy to set up and use.
- DynamoDB grows as the database expands, so the size does not have to be set.
- DynamoDB throughput will, however, need to be specific; this is how many reads and writes per second that are required. These are the Read capacity unit (RCU) and the Write capacity unit (WRU).
  - RCU = 1 strongly consistent read per second for an item of up to 4 kb in size.
  - RCU = 2 eventually consistent reads per second for an item of up to 4 kb in size.
  - WRU = 1 write per second for an item of up to 1 kb in size.
- You can find more information on Amazon DynamoDB at the following link.

https://docs.aws.amazon.com/dynamodb/

- Data Warehousing—Using Amazon Redshift
  - Redshift offers a sequel interface
  - Redshift if useful for analytical queries
  - Redshift if handy for computing aggregate numbers across an entire table.
  - You can find out more about Amazon Redshift at the following link(s).

https://docs.aws.amazon.com/redshift/index.html

Caching

For improved application performance without having to rewrite or redesign a programs core logic.

Caching can be performed at different levels, such as:

Web Level

For web level caching, AWS offers CloudFront, which is a content delivery network (CDN). CloudFront caches static content at an edge location that is closer to the system's users. This allows for faster application access time as the request does not have to go all the way back to the Amazon S3 servers.

When a user requests data that is not in the cache, the system will collect it from the Amazon S3 bucket, and that date will automatically be stored in the nearest location cache. The next time it is requested, the data will be retrieved from the cache.

More information and documentation on Amazon CloudFront can be found at the following link:

https://docs.aws.amazon.com/cloudfront/index.html

Application and Database Levels

Amazon offers ElastiCache to use between the database front end and database back end. The cache will collect items that are continuously requested of the master database to free up the processing power of the database and make retrieval times on the front end faster.

ElastiCache offers two types of caching options which it will set up for you:

- Memcached
  - Horizontal scaling is easy and can be done with Auto Discovery.
  - It allows for multithreading.
  - Memcached is a low maintenance option.
- Redis
  - Offers read replicas or failover.
  - It is a more sophisticated caching option of the two.
  - It offers support for data structures.
  - Has pub/sub messaging.

For more information on ElastiCache and its options, you can go to the following link(s).

https://docs.aws.amazon.com/elasticache/index.html

https://aws.amazon.com/elasticache/memcached/

https://aws.amazon.com/elasticache/redis/resources/

Solutions Designed for Scalability and Elasticity

In a well-architected design, no matter the content or how much traffic an application receives, it should be easy to scale them. If the traffic grows, the system should be able to scale up, and if it drops off, it should be able to scale down, which substantially improves the overall performance.

There are two types of AWS scaling:

- Horizontal scaling (scales in and out)
  - This is when the system grows depending on the number of instances required.
  - The system will add or remove instances as or when required.
- Vertical scaling (scales up and down)
  - This is when the system will replace the specifications of an instance.
  - This is used to allocate specifications such as more memory or more CPU.

Auto Scaling is the easiest way to scale instances as it can be launched across availability zones, can launch and terminate instances as or when needed. It can also register new instances with load balancers automatically.

Auto Scaling works in conjunction with an AWS monitoring service called CloudWatch. CloudWatch can be configured with certain instance thresholds that can be triggered when an instance exceeds the set parameters. These alarms will set the Auto Scaling Policies into action. These policies will determine the number of instances that need to be launched and what kind of instances to launch.

To learn how to correctly configure both CloudWatch and Auto Scaling, you can find more information at the following links.

https://docs.aws.amazon.com/autoscaling/index.html

https://aws.amazon.com/autoscaling/

https://docs.aws.amazon.com/cloudwatch/index.html

https://aws.amazon.com/cloudwatch/getting-started/

Determining High Performant Architectures

The best way to determine high performant architecture design for an AWS environment is to keep the following points in mind:

- Amazon S3 is the best storage solution for data that is unstructured.
- Always determine the database type and instance that is best for the required performance and workload.
- If there is a large workload that is constantly causing workflow blockages or failures, use caching. Caching can strategically improve system performance.
- Use Auto Scaling for the customers' advantage by knowing when and why to use the service.

Domain 2 Practice Test Questions

The following are a few practice exam questions to help test your knowledge.

Kindly note that all test questions were sourced from AWS (Exam Readiness: AWS Certified Solutions Architect, n.d.).

Practice Exam

Question 1:

From the list below, identify which features below to EBS.

Choose two out of four.

A. Amazon EBS volume can be encrypted.

B. Data stored on EBS is automatically replicated within an Availability Zone

C. Data on Amazon EBS volumes is lost when the attached instance is stopped

D. Amazon EBS data is automatically backed up to tape

Question 2:

For non-relational databases which is the best AWS Service:

Choose one out of four.

A. Amazon Glacier

B. Amazon DynamoDB

C. Amazon Redshift

D. Amazon RDS

Question 3:

Amazon ElastiCache supports which of the following cache engines?

Choose two out of four.

A. Memcached

B. Couchbase

C. MySQL

D. Redis

Question 4:

To launch a fully configured instantly, what is the template that Auto Scaling would use?

Choose one out of four.

A. User data

B. Launch configuration

C. Key pair

D. Instance type

Question 5:

Of the options below, which are characteristics of the AWS Auto Scaling Service?

Choose two out of six.

A. Collects and tracks metrics and sets alarms

B. Delivers push notifications

C. Sends traffic to healthy instances

D. Enforces a minimum number of running Amazon EC2 instances

E. Responds to changing conditions by adding or terminating Amazon EC2 instances.

F. Launches instances from a specified Amazon Machine Image (AMI).

Design High-Performing Architectures Test Question Answers

Answer to Question 1:

A. Amazon EBS volume can be encrypted.
B. Data stored on EBS is automatically replicated within an Availability Zone.

Answer to Question 2:

B. Amazon DynamoDB

Answer to Question 3:

A. Memcached
D. Redis

Answer to Question 4:

B. Launch configuration

Answer to Question 5:

D. Enforces a minimum number of running Amazon EC2 instances.
E. Responds to changing conditions by adding or terminating Amazon EC2 instances.
F. Launches instances from a specified Amazon Machine Image (AMI).

7. AWS Certified Solutions Architect Associate Test Questions

Read each question carefully and make sure you understand it before answering and moving on to the next one. An unanswered question is marked as incorrect and will negatively affect your overall score.

Here are 33 practice sample exam questions to help test your knowledge. Kindly note that these questions are sourced from ExamTopics (2020) and AWS Training and Certification (n.d.).

Question 1:

A mobile phone application runs statistical articles from individual files in an Amazon S3 bucket. There are articles older than 40 days that are no longer needed for the application and articles over 30 days old that are hardly ever read. These articles are no longer needed to be visible through the mobile application but must be archived for historical data purposes.

From the list below, select the cost-effective solution that best meets these requirements.

Choose one out of four.

A. For files older than 30 days, create lifecycle rules to move these files to Amazon S3 Standard Infrequent Access and use Amazon Glacier to move files older than 40 days to.

B. For files older than 30 days, create a Lambda function to move them to Amazon Glacier and move files older than 40 days to Amazon EBS.

C. Create a Lambda function that moves files to Amazon EBS that are older than 30 days and move files to Amazon Glacier that are older than 40 days.

D. For files older than 30 days, create lifecycle rules to move these files to Amazon Glacier and use Amazon S3 Standard Infrequent Access to move files older than 40 days to.

Question 2:

A company is launching an application that it expects to be very popular. The company needs a database that can scale with the rest of the application. The schema will change frequently. The application cannot afford any downtime for database changes.

Which AWS service allows the company to achieve these objectives?

Choose one out of four.

A. Amazon Aurora

B. Amazon RDS MySQL

C. Amazon Redshift

D. Amazon DynamoDB

Question 3:

A Solutions Architect is designing a new social media application. The application must provide a secure method for uploading profile photos. Each user should be able to upload a profile photo into a shared storage location for one week after their profile is created.

Which approach will meet all of these requirements?

Choose one out of four.

A. Use Amazon S3 with the default private access policy and generate pre-signed URLs each time a new site profile is created.

B. Use Amazon CloudFront with AWS CloudTrail for auditing the specific times when profile photos are uploaded.

C. Use Amazon EBS volumes with IAM policies restricting user access to specific time periods.

D. Use Amazon Kinesis with AWS CloudTrail for auditing the specific times when profile photos are uploaded.

Question 4:

A Solutions Architect needs to build a resilient data warehouse using Amazon Redshift. The Architect needs to rebuild the Redshift cluster in another region.

Which approach can the Architect take to address this requirement?

Choose one out of four.

A. Modify the Redshift cluster and configure the backup and specify the Amazon S3 bucket in the other region.

B. Modify the Redshift cluster and configure cross-region snapshots to the other region.

C. Modify the Redshift cluster to take snapshots of the Amazon EBS volumes each day, sharing those snapshots with the other region.

D. Modify the Redshift cluster to use AWS Snowball in export mode with data delivered to the other region.

Question 5:

A Solutions Architect is designing the architecture for a new three-tier web-based e-commerce site that must be available 24/7. Requests are expected to range from 100 to 10,000 each minute. Usage can vary depending on the time of day, holidays, and promotions. The design should be able to handle these volumes, with the ability to handle higher volumes if necessary.

How should the Architect design the architecture to ensure the web tier is cost-optimized and can handle the expected traffic?

Choose two out of five.

A. Use Amazon Route 53 to route traffic to the correct region.

B. Store all static files in a multi-AZ Amazon Aurora database.

C. Create a CloudFront distribution pointing to static content in Amazon S3.

D. Launch Amazon EC2 instances in an Auto Scaling group behind an ELB.

E. Use Amazon S3 multipart uploads to improve upload times.

Question 6:

An e-commerce application is hosted in AWS. The last time a new product was launched, the application experienced a performance issue due to an enormous spike in traffic. Management decided that capacity must be doubled the week after the product is launched.

Which is the most efficient way for management to ensure that capacity requirements are met?

Choose one out of four.

A. Add a Scheduled Scaling action

B. Add a Dynamic Scaling policy

C. Add a Step Scaling policy

D. Add Amazon EC2 Spot instances

Question 7:

A Solutions Architect is designing a solution that includes a managed VPN connection.

To monitor whether the VPN connection is up or down, the Architect should use:

Choose one out of four.

A. The CloudWatch TunnelState Metric.

B. An external service to ping the VPN endpoint from outside the VPC.

C. An AWS Lambda function that parses the VPN connection logs.

D. AWS CloudTrail to monitor the endpoint.

Question 8:

A Solutions Architect is designing a log-processing solution that requires storage that supports up to 500 MB/s throughput. The data is sequentially accessed by an Amazon EC2 instance.

Which Amazon storage type satisfies these requirements?

Choose one out of four.

A. EBS Cold HDD (sc1)

B. EBS Provisioned IOPS SSD (io1)

C. EBS General Purpose SSD (gp2)

D. EBS Throughput Optimized HDD (st1)

Question 9:

A Solutions Architect is designing network architecture for an application that has compliance requirements. The application will be hosted on Amazon EC2 instances in a private subnet and will be using Amazon S3 for storing data. The compliance requirements mandate that the data cannot traverse the public Internet.

What is the most secure way to satisfy this requirement?

Choose one out of four.

A. Use a NAT Instance

B. Use a VPC endpoint

C. Use a Virtual Private Gateway

D. Use a NAT Gateway

Question 10:

A company has a legacy application using a proprietary file system and plans to migrate the application to AWS.

Which storage service should the company use?

Choose one out four.

A. Amazon DynamoDB

B. Amazon S3

C. Amazon EBS

D. Amazon EFS

Question 11:

A company is launching a static website using the zone apex (mycompany.com). The company wants to use Amazon Route 53 for DNS.

Which steps should the company perform to implement a scalable and cost-effective solution?

Choose two out of five.

A. Host the website on an Amazon EC2 instance with ELB and Auto Scaling, and map a Route 53 alias record to the ELB endpoint.

B. Host the website using AWS Elastic Beanstalk, and map a Route 53 alias record to the Beanstalk stack.

C. Host the website on an Amazon EC2 instance, and map a Route 53 alias record to the public IP address of the Amazon EC2 instance.

D. Serve the website from an Amazon S3 bucket, and map a Route 53 alias record to the website endpoint.

E. Create a Route 53 hosted zone, and set the NS records of the domain to use Route 53 name servers.

Question 12:

A Solutions Architect is designing a new application that needs to access data in a different AWS account located within the same region. The data must not be accessed over the Internet.

Which solution will meet these requirements with the lowest cost?

Choose one out of four.

A. Add rules to the security groups in each account.

B. Establish a VPC Peering connection between accounts.

C. Configure Direct Connect in each account.

D. Add a NAT Gateway to the data account.

Question 13:

A Solutions Architect has a multi-layer application running in Amazon VPC. The application has an ELB Classic Load Balancer as the front end in a public subnet, and an Amazon EC2-based reverse proxy that performs content-based routing to two backend Amazon EC2 instances hosted in a private subnet. The Architect sees tremendous traffic growth and is concerned that the reverse proxy and current backend setup will be insufficient.

Which actions should the Architect take to achieve a cost-effective solution that ensures the application automatically scales to meet traffic demand?

Choose two out of five.

A. Replace the Amazon EC2 reverse proxy with an ELB internal Classic Load Balancer.

B. Add Auto Scaling to the Amazon EC2 backend fleet.

C. Add Auto Scaling to the Amazon EC2 reverse proxy layer.

D. Use t2 burstable instance types for the backend fleet.

E. Replace both the frontend and reverse proxy layers with an ELB Application Load Balancer.

Question 14:

A Solutions Architect plans to migrate NAT instances to NAT gateway. The Architect has NAT instances with scripts to manage high availability.

What is the most efficient method to achieve similar high availability with NAT gateway?

Choose one out of four.

A. Remove source/destination check on NAT instances.

B. Launch a NAT gateway in each Availability Zone.

C. Use a mix of NAT instances and NAT gateway.

D. Add an ELB Application Load Balancer in front of NAT gateway.

Question 15:

A Solutions Architect is designing a web application. The web and application tiers need to access the Internet, but they cannot be accessed from the Internet.

Which of the following steps is required?

Choose one out of four.

A. Attach an Elastic IP address to each Amazon EC2 instance and add a route from the private subnet to the public subnet.

B. Launch a NAT gateway in the public subnet and add a route to it from the private subnet.

C. Launch Amazon EC2 instances in the public subnet and change the security group to allow outbound traffic on port 80.

D. Launch a NAT gateway in the private subnet and deploy a NAT instance in the private subnet.

Question 16:

A Solutions Architect is designing a database solution that must support a high rate of random disk reads and writes. It must provide consistent performance, and requires long-term persistence.

Which storage solution best meets these requirements?

Choose one out of four.

A. An Amazon EBS Provisioned IOPS volume

B. An Amazon EBS General Purpose volume

C. An Amazon EBS Magnetic volume

D. An Amazon EC2 Instance Store

Question 17:

A Solutions Architect is designing a Lambda function that calls an API to list all running Amazon RDS instances.

How should the request be authorized?

Choose one out four.

A. Create an IAM access and secret key, and store it in the Lambda function.

B. Create an IAM role to the Lambda function with permissions to list all Amazon RDS instances.

C. Create an IAM role to Amazon RDS with permissions to list all Amazon RDS instances.

D. Create an IAM access and secret key, and store it in an encrypted RDS database.

Question 18:

An interactive, dynamic website runs on Amazon EC2 instances in a single subnet behind an ELB Classic Load Balancer.

Which design changes will make the site more highly available?

Choose one out four.

A. Move some Amazon EC2 instances to a subnet in a different way.

B. Move the website to Amazon S3.

C. Change the ELB to an Application Load Balancer.

D. Move some Amazon EC2 instances to a subnet in the same Availability Zone.

Question 19:

A Solutions Architect is about to deploy an API on multiple EC2 instances in an Auto Scaling group behind an ELB. The support team has the following operational requirements:

1. They get an alert when the requests per second go over 50,000.

2. They get an alert when latency goes over 5 seconds.

3. They can validate how many times a day users call the API requesting highly-sensitive data.

Which combination of steps does the Architect need to take to satisfy these operational requirements?

Choose two out five.

A. Ensure that CloudTrail is enabled.

B. Create a custom CloudWatch metric to monitor the API for data access.

C. Configure CloudWatch alarms for any metrics the support team requires.

D. Ensure that detailed monitoring for the EC2 instances is enabled.

E. Create an application to export and save CloudWatch metrics for longer-term trending analysis.

Question 20:

A Solutions Architect is designing a web application that is running on an Amazon EC2 instance. The application stores data in DynamoDB. The Architect needs to secure access to the DynamoDB table.

What combination of steps does AWS recommend to achieve secure authorization?

Choose two out of five.

A. Store an access key on the Amazon EC2 instance with rights to the DynamoDB table.

B. Attach an IAM user to the Amazon EC2 instance.

C. Create an IAM role with permissions to write to the DynamoDB table.

D. Attach an IAM role to the Amazon EC2 instance.

E. Attach an IAM policy to the Amazon EC2 instance.

Question 21:

A Solutions Architect is designing the storage layer for a production relational database. The database will run on Amazon EC2. The database is accessed by an application that performs intensive reads and writes, so the database requires the lowest random I/O latency.

Which data storage method fulfills the above requirements?

Choose one out of four.

A. Store data in a filesystem backed by Amazon Elastic File System (EFS).

B. Store data in Amazon S3 and use a third-party solution to expose Amazon S3 as a filesystem to the database server.

C. Store data in Amazon DynamoDB and emulate relational database semantics.

D. Stripe data across multiple Amazon EBS volumes using RAID 0.

Question 22:

A web application stores all data in an Amazon RDS Aurora database instance. A Solutions Architect wants to provide access to the data for a detailed report for the Marketing team but is concerned that the additional load on the database will affect the performance of the web application.

How can the report be created without affecting the performance of the application?

Choose one out of four.

A. Create a read replica of the database.

B. Provision of a new RDS instance as a secondary master.

C. Configure the database to be in multiple regions.

D. Increase the number of provisioned storage IOPS.

Question 23:

A company hosts a popular web application. The web application connects to a database running in a private VPC subnet. The web servers must be accessible only to customers on an SSL connection. The RDS MySQL database server must be accessible only from the web servers.

How should the Architect design a solution to meet the requirements without impacting running applications?

Choose one out of four.

A. Create a network ACL on the web server's subnet, and allow HTTPS inbound and MySQL outbound. Place both database and web servers on the same subnet.

B. Open an HTTPS port on the security group for web servers and set the source to 0.0.0.0/0. Open the MySQL port on the database security group and attach it to the MySQL instance. Set the source to Web Server Security Group.

C. Create a network ACL on the web server's subnet, and allow HTTPS inbound, and specify the source as 0.0.0.0/0. Create a network ACL on a database subnet, allow MySQL port inbound for web servers, and deny all outbound traffic.

D. Open the MySQL port on the security group for web servers and set the source to 0.0.0.0/0. Open the HTTPS port on the database security group and attach it to the MySQL instance. Set the source to Web Server Security Group.

Question 24:

A company's website receives 50,000 requests each second, and the company wants to use multiple applications to analyze the navigation patterns of the users on their website so that the experience can be personalized.

What can a Solutions Architect use to collect page clicks for the website and process them sequentially for each user?

Choose one out four.

A. Amazon Kinesis Stream

B. Amazon SQS standard queue

C. Amazon SQS FIFO queue

D. AWS CloudTrail trail

Question 25:

A company hosts a two-tier application that consists of a publicly accessible web server that communicates with a private database. Only HTTPS port 443 traffic to the web server must be allowed from the Internet.

Which of the following options will achieve these requirements?

Choose two out of five.

A. Security group rule that allows inbound Internet traffic for port 443.

B. Security group rule that denies all inbound Internet traffic except port 443.

C. Network ACL rule that allows port 443 inbound and all ports outbound for Internet traffic.

D. Security group rule that allows Internet traffic for port 443 in both inbound and outbound.

E. Network ACL rule that allows port 443 for both inbound and outbound for all Internet traffic.

Question 26:

A development team is building an application with front-end and back-end application tiers. Each tier consists of Amazon EC2 instances behind an ELB Classic Load Balancer. The instances run in Auto Scaling groups across multiple Availability Zones. The network team has allocated the 10.0.0.0/24 address space for this application. Only the front-end load balancer should be exposed to the Internet. There are concerns about the limited size of the address space and the ability of each tier to scale.

What should the VPC subnet design be in each Availability Zone?

Choose one out of four.

A. One public subnet for the load balancer tier, one public subnet for the front-end tier, and one private subnet for the backend tier.

B. One shared public subnet for all tiers of the application.

C. One public subnet for the load balancer tier and one shared private subnet for the application tiers.

D. One shared private subnet for all tiers of the application.

Question 27:

Legacy applications currently send messages through a single Amazon EC2 instance, which then routes the messages to the appropriate destinations. The Amazon EC2 instance is a bottleneck and single point of failure, so the company would like to address these issues.

Which services could address this architectural use case?

Choose two out of five.

A. Amazon SNS

B. AWS STS

C. Amazon SQS

D. Amazon Route 53

E. AWS Glue

Question 28:

A Solutions Architect needs to allow developers to have SSH connectivity to web servers. The requirements are as follows:

1. Limit access to users' origination from the corporate network.

2. Web servers cannot have SSH access directly from the Internet.

3. Web servers reside in a private subnet.

Which combination of steps must the Architect complete to meet these requirements?

Choose two out of five.

A. Create a bastion host that authenticates users against the corporate directory.

B. Create a bastion host with security group rules that only allow traffic from the corporate network.

C. Attach an IAM role to the bastion host with relevant permissions.

D. Configure the web servers' security group to allow SSH traffic from a bastion host.

E. Deny all SSH traffic from the corporate network in the inbound network ACL.

Question 29:

A company is designing a failover strategy in Amazon Route 53 for its resources between two AWS Regions. The company must have the ability to route a user's traffic to the region with the least latency, and if both regions are healthy, Route 53 should route traffic to resources in both regions.

Which strategy should the Solutions Architect recommend?

Choose one out four.

A. Configure active-active failover using Route 53 latency DNS records.

B. Configure active-passive failover using Route 53 latency DNS records.

C. Configure active-active failover using Route 53 failover DNS records.

D. Configure active-passive failover using Route 53 failover DNS records.

Question 30:

A company must collect temperature data from thousands of remote weather devices. The company must also store this data in a data warehouse to run aggregations and visualizations.

Which services will meet these requirements?

Choose two out of five.

A. Amazon Kinesis Data Firehouse

B. Amazon SQS

C. Amazon Redshift

D. Amazon SNS

E. Amazon DynamoDB

Question 31:

A company is implementing a data lake solution on Amazon S3. Its security policy mandates that the data stored in Amazon S3 should be encrypted at rest.

Which options can achieve this?

Choose two out of five.

A. Use SSL to encrypt the data while in transit to Amazon S3

B. Use S3 server-side encryption with customer-provided keys (SSE-C).

C. Use S3 bucket policies to restrict access to the data at rest.

D. Use client-side encryption before ingesting the data to Amazon S3 using encryption keys.

E. Use S3 server-side encryption with an Amazon EC2 key pair.

Question 32:

An online retailer has a series of flash sales occurring every Friday. Sales traffic will increase during the sales only and the platform will handle the increased load.

The platform is a three-tier application. The web tier runs on Amazon EC2 instances behind an Application Load Balancer. Amazon CloudFront is used to reduce web server load, but many requests for dynamic content must go to the web servers.

What should be done to the web tier to reduce costs without impacting performance or reliability?

Choose one out of four.

A. Use Spot Instances.

B. Implement Amazon ElastiCache.

C. Purchase scheduled Reserved Instances.

D. Use T-series instances.

Question 33:

A Solutions Architect is designing the architecture for a web application that will be hosted on AWS. Internet users will access the application using HTTP and HTTPS.

How should the Architect design the traffic control requirements?

Choose one out of four.

A. Use a network ACL to allow outbound ports for HTTP and HTTPS. Deny other traffic for inbound and outbound.

B. Use a network ACL to allow inbound ports for HTTP and HTTPS. Deny other traffic for inbound and outbound.

C. Allow inbound ports for HTTP and HTTPS in the security group used by the web servers.

D. Allow outbound ports for HTTP and HTTPS in the security group used by the web servers.

AWS Certified Solutions Architect Associate Test Questions Answers

Answer to Question 1:

A. For files older than 30 days, create lifecycle rules to move these files to Amazon S3 Standard Infrequent Access and use Amazon Glacier to move files older than 40 days to.

Answer to Question 2:

C. Amazon Redshift

Answer to Question 3:

A. Use Amazon S3 with the default private access policy and generate pre-signed URLs each time a new site profile is created.

Answer to Question 4:

C. Modify the Redshift cluster to take snapshots of the Amazon EBS volumes each day, sharing those snapshots with the other region.

Answer to Question 5:

C. Create a CloudFront distribution pointing to static content in Amazon S3.

D. Launch Amazon EC2 instances in an Auto Scaling group behind an ELB.

Answer to Question 6:

B. Add a Dynamic Scaling policy

Answer to Question 7:

A. the CloudWatch TunnelState Metric

Answer to Question 8:

D. EBS Throughput Optimized HDD (st1)

Answer to Question 9:

B. Use a VPC endpoint

Answer to Question 10:

C. Amazon EBS

Answer to Question 11:

C. Host the website on an Amazon EC2 instance, and map a Route 53 alias record to the public IP address of the Amazon EC2 instance.

D. Serve the website from an Amazon S3 bucket, and map a Route 53 alias record to the website endpoint.

Answer to Question 12:

B. Establish a VPC Peering connection between accounts.

Answer to Question 13:

A. Replace the Amazon EC2 reverse proxy with an ELB internal Classic Load Balancer.

B. Add Auto Scaling to the Amazon EC2 backend fleet.

Answer to Question 14:

B. Launch a NAT gateway in each Availability Zone.

Answer to Question 15:

B. Launch a NAT gateway in the public subnet and add a route to it from the private subnet.

Answer to Question 16:

A. An Amazon EBS Provisioned IOPS volume

Answer to Question 17:

C. Create an IAM role to Amazon RDS with permissions to list all Amazon RDS instances.

Answer to Question 18:

A. Move some Amazon EC2 instances to a subnet in a different way.

Answer to Question 19:

B. Create a custom CloudWatch metric to monitor the API for data access.

D. Ensure that detailed monitoring for the EC2 instances is enabled.

Answer to Question 20:

C. Create an IAM role with permissions to write to the DynamoDB table.

D. Attach an IAM role to the Amazon EC2 instance.

Answer to Question 21:

D. Stripe data across multiple Amazon EBS volumes using RAID 0.

Answer to Question 22:

B. Provision a new RDS instance as a secondary master.

Answer to Question 23:

B. Open an HTTPS port on the security group for web servers and set the source to 0.0.0.0/0. Open the MySQL port on the database security group and attach it to the MySQL instance. Set the source to the Web Server Security Group.

Answer to Question 24:

A. Amazon Kinesis Stream

Answer to Question 25:

A. Security group rule that allows inbound Internet traffic for port 443.

E. Network ACL rule that allows port 443 for both inbound and outbound for all Internet traffic.

Answer to Question 26:

A. One public subnet for the load balancer tier, one public subnet for the front-end tier, and one private subnet for the backend tier.

Answer to Question 27:

A. Amazon SNS

C. Amazon SQS

Answer to Question 28:

A. Create a bastion host that authenticates users against the corporate directory.

C. Attach an IAM role to the bastion host with relevant permissions.

Answer to Question 29:

A. Configure active-active failover using Route 53 latency DNS records.

Answer to Question 30:

A. Amazon Kinesis Data Firehouse

B. Amazon SQS

Answer to Question 31:

C. Use S3 bucket policies to restrict access to the data at rest.

E. Use S3 server-side encryption with an Amazon EC2 key pair.

Answer to Question 32:

C. Purchase scheduled Reserved Instances.

Answer to Question 33:

C. Allow inbound ports for HTTP and HTTPS in the security group used by the web servers.

Conclusion

Amazon is providing a lot of web services. Many of them are stated above in the book.

Cloud computing, in the simplest terms, means storing and processing data and services over the Internet, rather than the hard drive of your computer.

Your hard disk is what cloud computing isn't about. That's called local storage and computing when you store data on–or run programs from the hard drive. Anything you need is physically close to you, which means you have fast and easy access to your data (for that one device, or those on the local network). Operating off the hard drive is how the tech industry has been operating for a decade.

The future of computing technology lies in the cloud. Which means that if you're not adapting your company to suit the cloud model your company will be left behind in this world of modern technology.

Cloud computing is when organizations share a network of freely accessible servers. Servers are stored on the Internet, allowing companies to handle data "in the cloud" instead of on a local server. It is a virtual space in which devices on the network can access data from anywhere.

Amazon Web Services (AWS) Introduction to Famous Amazon Web Services is a robust cloud platform developed by Amazon's e-commerce giant. It offers software-as - a-Service (SaaS), platform-as - a-Service (PaaS), and infrastructure-as - a-Service (IaaS) services. Think about the history of the electricity supply to grasp the logic of AWS.

Initially, factories will build their own plants to fuel their own facilities. Over time, governments and private investors have developed large power plants that supply electricity to numerous towns, factories, and homes. Under this new model, the factories will pay even less per unit of power due to the economies of scale enjoyed by the massive power plants. AWS was designed and built on the basis of a similar logic.

Amazon Web Services offers cloud infrastructure from hundreds of data centers and numerous availability zones (AZs) spanning regions of the world. Every AZ includes a number of data centers. Customers can set up virtual machines and duplicate their data in several AZs in order to provide a highly scalable network that is resistant to server failure or data center failure.

With AWS, all you get is instances with different CPU resource configurations, memory, storage, and networking. Each model is available in various sizes to accommodate the workload as needed. The instances come from Amazon Machine Images (AMI). Such computer images function as a prototype that configures the operating system and defines the user's operating environment. Users may also set up their own AMIs.

www.ingramcontent.com/pod-product-compliance
Lightning Source LLC
LaVergne TN
LVHW082354200926
848481LV00012B/3560